The Backyard Horseman

The Backyard Horseman

Ron Rude

Mountain Press Publishing Co.
Missoula, 1987

Copyright © 1987
Mountain Press Publishing Co.

Library of Congress Cataloging in Publication Data

Rude, Ron, 1943—
  The backyard horseman.

  Bibliography: p.141
  Includes index.
  1. Horses.   2. Horsemanship.   I. Title.
SF285.R86   1987   636.1   87-11187
ISBN 0-87842-211-0 (pbk.)

135798642

MOUNTAIN PRESS PUBLISHING CO.
P.O. Box 2399 ● Missoula, MT 59601

Dedication

To my dad and his dad . . . horsemen both

Note to female readers:

I write in the masculine gender out of habit and a need for efficiency, not to ignore women equestrians. In fact, though some of the top horsemen in the world are still men, I think it is the women who will dominate this activity eventually. At least in my experience, women are more patient, open-minded, and perseverant than modern men in dealing with horses, and they seem to have a more genuine interest in the welfare of horses.

Acknowledgements

Sincere thanks go to:

Bob Fundingsland and his JR Boot and
  Saddle store
Western Outdoors and Hook's Saddlery
Crag Mountain Arabians (Larry Bailey
  Stables)
Dr. Bob Gregg of Lynch Creek Veterinary
  Clinic
Kathy McEldry
Kalispell, Montana's One Hour Fast
  Photo (I don't even know the names of
  the folks there who took such good care
  of my photos)
Multitudes of writers and horsemen
  whose names and locations I've long
  forgotten, but who taught me what I
  know
My wife Karen and sons Steve, Jeff, and
  Mark, for tolerating my fascination
  with horses

Introduction

So you're one of those people who can't resist a peek at horse books. Welcome . . . you're in good company.

Perhaps you're browsing because you're thinking about buying a first horse or thinking about "getting back into horses" after years of growing up and making a living. Perhaps you've recently bought a horse, but ownership is more troublesome than you thought it would be. Or perhaps you're the sort of horse lover who always wants to know more about your favorite topic. If, in addition to any of these, you have limited space and a limited budget for your horse activities, this book was written for you.

What can you expect to gain from these pages?

You can learn enough to get a safe and sensible start in small-scale horse ownership, and you may find ways and reasons to make that start grow into serious horsemanship. Some chapters contain all you really need to know on a particular aspect of horsemanship; other chapters are the subject of entire books (I'll suggest some of these along the way). Still other chapters can only touch on things that require a lifetime of study.

This is as much a why-to book as it is a how-to book. In fact, the whole first chapter is devoted to rearranging your thinking before you become actively involved with horses. And there are some horse stories I hope will illustrate the points I'm preaching.

Why should you believe what I tell you?

Perhaps a little autobiography will answer that.

I am a "backyard horseman." I do not make a living with horses, although I sometimes earn a few dollars training and shoeing. I keep three horses on five acres near a small town in western Montana where I teach high school English. My wife is a homemaker. As I write this, our three sons are teenagers. I like to read, write, hunt, hike, travel, and eat. I enjoy the company of my wife, my sons, a few close friends, and many acquaintances, including hundreds of former students. For reasons I can't fully explain, horses have been my consuming avocation since early childhood. I've tried jogging, guitar-playing, wood carving, graduate school, a variety of part-time jobs; they all fall away, and I'm back to horses. As a matter of fact, the only thing I would give up horses for is my family. That's not overblown sentimentalism or romanticism, nor is it an attempt to ease my conscience; it is simply a fact of my life.

I started riding my grandfather's workhorses when I was about seven. In the late '40s a few farmers still harvested with teams, and I remember those big horses–shrouded in fly nets, munching gallons of oats at noon breaks–more vividly than much of the rest of my childhood.

My first pony arrived when I was ten, my first saddle horses during my adolescence. By that time I was reading everything I could about horses, and daydreaming of the time when I would do nothing but roam untracked forests on horseback. I was also convinced I already knew it all.

In 1962 I had a summer job on the Van Cleve guest ranch near Big Timber, Montana. I milked the cows, chopped wood, and guided guests on short horseback rides. In 1965 I was back for more, this time doing nothing but riding. I averaged fifty or more hours per week on horseback, and I learned a great deal. The most important lesson was that horsemanship was much bigger and more complicated than I had ever expected, and the fact that I knew how to saddle up and ride wasn't even kindergarten stuff. It took many more years, however, for that lesson to really sink in.

After college, three years of Uncle Sam's Army, and a couple of one-year teaching positions, I came to my present home. I had no horsemanship plan, but I continued to read, experiment, boast, make a fool of myself, make more mistakes, and, gradually, learn some things about horses.

Today I break and school a few colts, take pack trips into the mountains, occasionally work cattle for ranchers, and help other riders who are having trouble with their horses. I get these things done with a minimum of pain and problems for myself or my horses. I don't spend as much time working my horses as I would like nor as much as I should.

These experiences shape my point of

view. I am not a professional trainer, nor do I raise horses, nor do I show them. I do not know all the answers, nor even all the questions. But I do know what it is to be a backyard horseman; I do know some shortcuts; I do know some ways to enjoy more and hurt less. It is these things I want to pass along to you.

This book proceeds with certain assumptions: that you either have a horse or plan to get one (or more) no matter the obstacles; that you either cannot or will not spend a major portion of your income on horses; that you have never done full-time horse work for a living.

I ask that you do not read this book just looking for interesting tidbits. Instead, study it, think about it, and read it again; I ask that you do the same with at least a half-dozen other horsemanship books.

I ask that when you do get a horse you spend plenty of time applying your reading and gaining the experience that will round out that reading. I ask that you form a plan and set some goals for the horse and for yourself. Purposeless ownership is a dead end that causes both people and horses a long list of griefs.

Finally, I ask that you be open-minded about ideas which differ from those you now hold, and I ask that you be objective about your own level of experience.

You see, professional horse people are rightfully a little scornful of us backyard types. They make profits and progress while we often do neither. They earn ribbons and trophies while we embarrass ourselves. Their horses are healthy and active while ours are often apathetic and ill-mannered. With a few subtle signals, they get more performance from their horses than we do with a flurry of kicks, curses, arm-waving, and excuse-making.

But we can gain rapidly on these professionals if we want to, because failure to honestly evaluate our own abilities and use our time intelligently are the only real barriers between us and them. The main goal of this book is to help you remove those barriers, and to help you see that real progress comes from the understanding that horsemanship isn't just owning and riding a horse.

Contents

chapter one
Some Myths About Horsemanship

We horse-lovers first get into trouble because our perception of horsemanship diverges from reality. Maybe this divergence began when as children we read those romantic horse books . . . who can forget the adventure as a boy, miraculously freed of parental rule, conquers nasty Arabs, ocean storms, desert distance, upsets, and fear, to ride to victory on his true friend the Black Stallion.

The trouble with reading such stories, however, is that for some reason we remember the Black and forget old What's-His-Name, the milkman's delivery nag living in the same barn. He's the one who plods the same boring route every day, comes home to his dingy stall every night, and lays in his own manure. Somehow, when we begin thinking about owning a horse, we think it's going to be all Black Stallion and no old What's-His-Name.

I assume that if you're reading about horses, you already have a list of reasons for owning them. But if you find your reasons in the following list of delusions, perhaps you too have some unrealistic perceptions of what horsemanship will be.

Delusion #1: "My horse will love me because I will be kind to him. I won't have any trouble with him and all our moments together will be of the most intimate and exciting kind."

Like the Black Stallion myth, this notion is generated by books and movies. Your horse may indeed seem to love you, at least at feeding time. But really, he has his own agenda at all times. If you doubt that, turn him loose in a thousand acres, see if he then prefers you to his freedom and his herd. You'll go home sadder, wiser, and alone.

Horses are creatures of fairly simple needs. None of these needs involves building a meaningful relationship with a demanding biped who creates fences and saddles.

Delusion #2: "One horse is enough, and he won't cost much to keep."

If you consider only the cost of the cheapest horse and one winter's hay, you could be right. If you are a little more realistic, if you figure in the cost of land, fences, equipment, transportation, veterinarians, shoeing, a second horse and his feed—no horse likes to be alone, just as no rider does for long—you can see the tally growing. Never believe one will be enough. Never believe horses are a cheap hobby.

Delusion #3: "I'll get a couple of horses to keep the weeds down." A variation of this is "Horses are harmless, and they don't need much room."

Horses will take care of your weeds certainly. One horse will eat a couple of acres of weeds and grass to dusty death in a month. The weeds that survive will be inedible by man or beast. While it is possible and even practical sometimes to keep horses in a limited space, a horse needs much more space that you do, and will be unhappy without it.

Delusion #4: "I plan to raise horses for a profit."

There's a saying in my part of the country: It's possible to make a small fortune raising horses, if you start with a large fortune. I suspect this is the case everywhere for the small operator.

The people who do make money with horses do so in a couple of ways. One, they use a red-ink horse operation as a write-off for other investments. The IRS, by the way, is pretty sharp about spotting these. Two,

they invest a major share of their time and earnings in horses, and that investment, along with some luck, has given them a high-quality stallion or a few performance horses that pay for the rest of the business. The small-time owner cannot profit because he has neither the time, nor the space, nor, usually, the initial capital to do so.

Delusion #5: "I'll enjoy horses because I need something to do with my spare time."

Seriously now, how much spare time are you talking about? Hours per week? Empty Sunday afternoons? So far, you don't have enough to do your horses justice, particularly if you are a beginner. If you knock out all those days when the weather is bad or you have a cold or company is coming, all those evenings when the sun dies at five or the kids need transportation, you don't have any time for horses at all.

Delusion #6: "I've been around horses ever since childhood. I'll break and train one for myself."

If you're harboring this idea, take a hard look at your experience. It takes much more experience to break a horse well, to give him the basics without hampering his eventual learning of more complex tasks, than it does just to ride him. Anyone with a little guts can climb on the average colt a few times, jerk his face this·way and that, and declare him broke to ride. But he will be at a dead end if the rider does just those things. To break and school horses, you need first to have ridden enough finished horses to know what kinds of things you want and don't want, what kinds of things a good horse knows. Somewhere you need to have learned the myriad little tricks and the progression of training that bring a horse to that well-broke state. All of this isn't something you know by virtue of having ridden when you were younger. The fact that you learned to read doesn't mean you're ready to write *A Tale of Two Cities*.

When I was seventeen I just knew I could break anything with four legs, so I climbed on Flip, a two-year-old, out in a mucky swamp where he couldn't buck too hard. It worked. The muck kept him docile; it also strained some muscles so he was stiff and weak for a long time. Eventually I was back at him again, galloping madly about the pastures, convinced that once he learned to stop, he was broke. He did stop finally. Ran smack into a tree with his forehead and knocked himself to his knees. Crude, but effective for the moment. Flip couldn't, however, make the connection and never did learn to stop on command. I blamed his lack of brains, of course, but I should have blamed my own.

Delusion #7: "I'll buy a baby horse and raise him. That's cheaper, and we'll be such good friends that breaking him will be a cinch."

No it isn't; no it won't.

Raising a colt involves many risks. Illness, fences, dogs, cars, and freak accidents can kill or cripple your colt long before he is ridable. One day a friend of mine noticed oats dribbling out the bottom of his yearling's jaw. Feel on yourself, right along the jawbone where your tongue is lashed down. Something big had sliced clear through and food was falling out. Repairable, yes, but it left a permanent lump. And this happened in a clean pasture from an unknown object, which still lurks there.

In addition to the risks, remember that a horse can only take a little light work at age two and really isn't ready for hard work until five. All those years you'll be feeding, cleaning, worming, worrying, and waiting. At the end, there's no guarantee a house-pet colt will be easier to break and train. In fact, pets are often more difficult because they have no fear of, and thus no respect for, their owner.

I once broke a three-year-old stud colt that had been raised alone in a barn since weaning, fed the best hay and grain daily, and treated like the king of the castle. When I got him he was a kicking, striking, biting, pawing, prancing spoiled brat. Much of this was attributable to too much good grain and some typical young stallion behavior. But a good share of it was from never having been subject to the wrath of older horses in a herd; nor had he been subject to the forcefulness of a knowledgeable owner. In the several weeks I spent breaking him, he was sullen and lazy. The last I heard of him he had carried his owner through a barbed-wire fence in a sudden, mad attack on two old geldings in a neighboring pasture.

Raising horses isn't much different than training them in one sense: the risks are very high, and you need to know what you are doing.

Delusion #8: "I don't need to learn all that fancy stuff like leads and collection. I'll just get a horse and ride him."

I spent the first ten years of my horse-owning career frozen in this position. Then one afternoon a teen-aged girl, trying out a horse of mine, said I was asking too much money for an "essentially green-broke" horse. I had spent two years riding that horse and had put everything I knew into her. My thoughts about that girl are unprintable. But a year later I visited the horse. It's manners, training, and physical conditioning under the girl's care were so far above anything I had ever produced that it darn near destroyed my manhood.

The point is, of course, that the "fancy stuff" is the essence of true riding skill. Without study and practice, you aren't a horseman, you're just a rider, and you're at a standstill.

Delusion #9: "Kids and horses just naturally go together."

The photos of Mom, Dad, and shiny kids all on horseback, or the photos of Sis holding her first barrel-racing ribbon and wearing the world's biggest tinsel smile all reinforce this myth. These things do happen. But think for a moment about what has gone on behind the scenes to make these photos happen.

For a family of four to ride well-bred, well-broke horses means a minimum of $5000 invested in horseflesh and gear and much more in peripheral items. Add in the fact that the day the photograph was taken was the only day all year when jobs, school, dental appointments, sports, relatives, and the weather cooperated simultaneously, and you can understand why the event was worth a picture.

This kids-and-horses myth needs more examination than the rest, so bear with me a moment. Begin by asking: why am I really getting a horse for my child?

One reason might be that you, Mom or Dad, want a horse but feel a little silly saying so. Consequently, you've decided that it's the kids who want one. If you can justify the whole program financially, and if nobody else notices that it's you who gets all the fun out of the deal, it might just work.

Still, this scenario reminds me of when I was ten and bought my mother a 3-pound replica of a Colt .45 for her birthday. It wasn't exactly what she had in mind for her charm bracelet and (surprise, surprise) she let me keep it for her in the old leather holster I already owned.

Another possibility, one I've had to squelch in myself, is the temptation for a horse-loving parent to force horses onto the children. This might net you a whole house full of expert young riders, but it might backfire. You might be fighting kids for riding time, or you might be fighting to make them ride at all. You'll feel obligated to make it work, but it may be unworkable. You may be dead wrong to demand this unessential activity from kids who want something else; you are certainly wrong if you cause an endless family squabble. Good horsemanship needs to begin in honesty; if the kids aren't really interested, you shouldn't use them as the excuse.

Still another possibility is that you think it might be a nice thing for the kids to have a horse. Owning a horse can be nice, but it is also much more complex than owning a motorcycle, for example. There is too much at stake, particularly from the horse's point of view.

It is also possible that your child asked for a horse and, with the persistence children have, begged until you were ready to give in. Don't give in just yet. Has your child wanted other major things, received them, used them, and forgotten them? If so, it doesn't mean there is something wrong with the child, nor does it mean there is something wrong with your performance as a parent. In fact, things are as normal as can be. But a horse has needs that must be met daily as long as you own it. Will a horse hold your child's interest long enough to make this long-term investment worthwhile?

A family I know went through this problem. Their young daughter desperately wanted a horse. But, there was no room and no time, so the parents refused, year after year. Long before the daughter left for college, her horse-interest had been forgotten.

It is possible, of course, that your child will develop a serious interest in horses. If that happens and if you have the resources, you should indulge him or her. But remember: only a small percentage of kids who think they like horses will actually use those horses over a long period of time. Even in the most horse-loving families, not every child will be interested. A child who pursues his or her interests without parental push is rare, and even the self-motivated child will require a great deal of your time.

Think about kids in three age groups for a few moments:

From infancy through age seven, kids can easily be frightened or hurt by horses and ponies. Also, these kids can't be left unsupervised, since they can't handle the animals, equipment, and countless tiny emergencies that arise with horses. Young children think of horses mainly as an extension of the fun and affection they expect from a parent rather than as an end in themselves. They will often be happier and safer riding behind a parent's saddle than having their own horse or pony.

From ages eight through twelve, things change rapidly. These kids are mature enough to learn quickly, and many are ready for horses. Some are ready to compete in shows or other events, and they will become skilled in a short time. But they are still immature enough to become easily bored with any routine, and they cannot be left solely responsible for horse care, training schedules, or, of course, transportation. Whatever the level of activity for the eight-through-twelve group, there will still have to be much parental supervision and support, in addition to the guidance of professional instructors.

If you involve eight- through twelve-year-old children in competition, you need to ask yourself whether you really want them subjected to activities often dominated by parents who will spend whatever it takes to snatch little blue ribbons away from other parents. For too many parents, kids' competition is an extension of their own egos, and every mistake children make is a chunk torn from parental identity. It isn't only the hapless children that suffer; horses do, too. As pressure builds it is easy for children and parents to needlessly jerk, whack, and spur the horses, which frequently are even less prepared for the events than the children.

On the other hand, kids who learn to compete hard, lose gracefully, and win humbly gain valuable social and personal skills, and they develop the easy self-confidence of the truly strong personality.

A few kids between thirteen and eighteen can become so competent they frighten adults. They can become the kind of student, athlete, musician, or horseman their parents dreamed of being. But, these are the mature and dedicated few. The rest are the normal majority for whom puberty shows up three years late and algebra three years early, the boys who prop up wobbly manhood with deeds of meaningless risk, the girls who cannot push the control button on pin ball moods. They still need prompting about every aspect of their daily lives, including horse care. They need attention and affection as much as they need more responsibility, because their self-esteem is still eggshell thin. Horses may help or hinder their growing up; which one is up to the parents as much as the adolescent.

Would your kids just naturally go together with horses? I can't answer that for you, but perhaps you can consider the question more objectively. Assuming you will buy horses for your kids, here are a few practical hints.

1. Find a way to give the child frequent riding lessons for a couple of years before you invest in horses.

2. Assess your resources objectively (time, money, space, patience, courage, persistence, health) before you buy.

3. Set realistic goals with your child, and keep pushing toward those goals.

You want a horse? Start with a long period of self-examination. If you can pass the exam, you might just be off to a good start.

chapter two
Stewardship

For several years, futurists have predicted that rising populations and shrinking farmland will inevitably collide to produce food shortages. So far, this hasn't happened, mainly because of the efficiency of modern farming methods. But there is no doubt that farmland, rangeland, and the more marginally productive wildlife winter ranges are being plowed under for highways, industrial plots, and housing developments. Small-time horsemen are right in the thick of it all, buying acreages out of town, then watching in dismay as town marches out to swallow them.

Development isn't likely to stop, even when wage increases slow and interest rates climb, since owning land is part of the American Dream. Country living symbolizes independence and self-sufficiency, and it is here to stay in some form until economics or lack of space make it impossible.

Backyard horsemen like myself, who enjoy the blessings of semi-rural living, are contributors to the problem too. We are, after all, taking up land that could often be producing food directly or indirectly, and our horses don't contribute much to the stability of the national economy. Probably the only horsemen who aren't a problem in this sense are those who use horses for productive work.

Using land for our horses isn't as wasteful as many other uses. Pasture kept in reasonable condition could produce food for humans should the need arise. The land hasn't been stripped of its topsoil and covered with asphalt, nor has it become a toxic waste dump bubbling and oozing its poisons into our grandchildren's lives. Furthermore, horses don't burn fossil fuels. Horses and their effluents are degradable. Horses don't contribute to noise pollution as do snowmobiles, boats, dirt bikes, or all-terrain vehicles. Horsemen don't need to wallow in guilt.

But our land is out of production, and it can only be put back into production if we treat it well. For the sake of our consciences and for later generations, we have a duty to take care of it.

It isn't an easy job. Horses confined are as destructive as any domestic animal except pigs. They crop the grass so close they have to move their lips aside to get their teeth on the tiny blades. They will jerk roots out and cheerfully munch these as well as the grass itself. Shod hooves cut the first inch of soil, crushing plants and turning up fragile roots. Horses' weight over a long period compacts the soil and makes life even tougher for young plants. Where horses make their paths and kill vegetation, erosion sets in. Horse urine is so strong it can kill back grass for weeks. Worm medicine expelled in droppings leaches into the soil. Only the toughest weeds—those so noxious that horses don't touch them—survive, and these spread quickly to neighboring land.

Watch a grazing horse and you will notice that he takes a bite or two, moves one foot, takes another bite, moves another foot. In the wild, horses, like other grazing animals, keep on the move and on good range do far less damage than when we confine them.

Free-ranging horses might not cover the same spot of grass more than a couple of times per year. But when we confine horses their destructive capabilities gallop into view. It isn't their fault; it is our fault and therefore our problem.

We can lessen the impact. First, we shouldn't keep more horses than we actually use. Several horses for each family member might be nice, but if only two people ride frequently, common sense says we should have only two horses. When I was younger we moved to a forty-acre farmstead, half woods and half meadow, adjoined by considerably more pasture land, which we leased. Our initial horse herd consisted of three mares. A few years later we had nearly a dozen horses of various ages, most not even broke to ride. They ate twenty or more tons of hay each winter and kept our pastures chewed flat from April through October. Only good soil and tough Minnesota sod kept us from ruining that place. True, it was fun to watch a dozen horses race across the meadows, especially with the babies flitting in and out of the herd. But good stewardship? Definitely not. The original three mares would have been enough.

Besides keeping the size of their herds down, horsemen can rotate pastures. Even where your pastures are only a few acres,

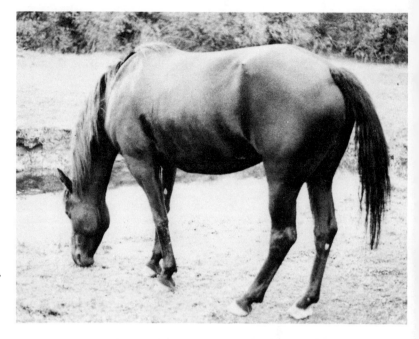

Without thoughtful management, grazing horses can turn lush pasture into a desert.

those acres can be fenced in half and used sparingly. Horses eat much more than they need if you let them, and consequently should be shut away from food during daylight hours. If your land is small, say two acres or less, your horses may have to be penned all the time. In strictly economic terms, this is far cheaper anyway, since hay at a few hundred dollars per year will never match the cost of land.

Hillside and forest land, which are being developed as the flatter farm land is filled, present new problems. There is less topsoil, so the owner is obligated to take what erosion control measures he can. This may mean particularly good care of sod conditions, or it may mean keeping horses confined at all times. In forest land, horses will destroy trees by stamping out the roots in a few favorite spots. They will eat bark and these trees, too, will die. Also, you'll have to cut down trees to give your horses sunlight, since they need that commodity as much as you do. Forested land grows very little grass, so what feed is available will be overgrazed.

If you live uphill from nearby homes, you'll be obligated to keep your horse facilities particularly sanitary, so urine and manure don't contaminate water sources below. (Still another consideration in hill country, though it has nothing to do with stewardship, is that horses are helpless on

ice. If your pens tilt much, your horses will be on dangerous footing all winter.)

In dry country, which includes most of the West, an irrigation system will provide more pasture and can, if handled properly, improve soil quality. But irrigation can speed depletion of the soil too, since close grazing and constant weathering remove nutrients in two directions. One answer is fertilizer, of course, but this is an expensive, short-term solution. You'll need at least a hundred pounds per acre per year at approximately $15 per hundred pounds. Your country agent can tell you the right type to use. Another answer is to allow grass to grow tall early in the summer, mow it down, and not allow grazing until grass has regrown several inches tall. This makes a natural mulch, although it isn't as good as what Mother Nature does; she lets a full crop die and rot each year.

A still better option is the practice of allowing no grazing one year, grazing half of the following year, and grazing the whole season of the third year. This cycle can be repeated indefinitely, although it won't work for small plots. If you have fifteen or twenty acres and can restrain yourself to keeping only a few animals, it will work well.

Good stewardship starts with care of your land, but it doesn't end there. Good stewardship involves such little things as finding a sanitary way to dispose of horse

manure and keeping the fly population down to avoid antagonizing the neighbors. It means maintaining horse-proof fences so the neighbors don't have to live in fear and loathing of your garden-eating pets. It involves respect for others' property, shown by not cutting across their corners, by asking permission to cross their land, by sending an occasional thank-you note.

Stewardship includes self-respect too. The appearance of our facilities counts. We need to look at our neighborhoods to see whether our home and horse facility are up to snuff. When we keep horses amidst broken boards, old car bodies, sagging barbed wire, tumbled-down shelters, falling gates, garbage cans, moldy hay, and fluttering pieces of plastic, we create a poor impression of ourselves and of horsemen in general. Repairing, painting, and general beautifying aren't pretentious; they merely reflect good mental health and good stewardship.

When we leave home, too, we must consider the impact we and our horses are having. Some of the worst land abuse is found on public lands where careless horsemen have let their animals trample vegetation. Using fewer animals and being more thoughtful can prevent these things. If we are careless, we have no one but ourselves to blame when backpackers,

ecological purists, and government officials bargain to ban horses from public land. Disrespect is also evident when we leave dirty stalls at the fairgrounds, bring unruly dogs to a gathering of horses, ride a stallion when event organizers have asked us not to, or run our horses when trail-ride etiquette says we should not. Whether we prefer wilderness or civilization, minimum impact should be a touchstone of our horse activities.

Stewardship also involves thinking objectively about the kind and quantity of natural resources we use in our horse outfits. We don't need the world's largest trailers nor the skin of endangered species on our boots. If this sounds like the deluded mutterings of a back-to-nature zealot, reflect on the notion that what we choose not to use is also a measure of our dedication to true horsemanship.

I'm not advocating that Americans live under a black cloud of guilt about our collective wealth. It is true that we have much comfort and opportunity, true that in some places the price of this book would feed a family for a week, true that what we spend to feed our horses and other pets could buy food for other humans. But like people in even the most destitute of places, we cannot live happily without dreams and plans. If those dreams mean land and horses, so be it.

On the other hand, let's remember that having dreams and the wherewithal to realize them doesn't give us the right to leave a mess for later generations. Land is the basis of our lives. In our rapidly urbanizing culture, we have lost track of this truth, but it is truth nonetheless. What we do with land, whether the whole nation or our own little plot, is one criterion by which our children will judge us. Horsemen have as much responsibility in this as anyone else because we engage in an activity that is so inextricably tied to the earth.

chapter three
Equipment and Maintenance

As you page through the tack catalogues, it appears that there is no end to what you need to buy. But the same scary possibility exists in most other recreational areas, and while for most activities there are plenty of frills available, you can also get by nicely with the basics. You need those basic items, however, and they must be of good quality. In the hardware store, it's tempting to pick up a set of screwdrivers from the "any 3 for $1" bin, but we know from experience that the first time the tool is really needed it will fail us. The same is true of horse gear. Good equipment is seldom cheap. Cheap equipment is seldom good.

Initial purchase prices aren't the only expense. Keeping that equipment in good shape requires time and work. It seems contradictory to complain about purchase prices while ignoring the maintenance that prevents further purchasing. Failure to maintain horse equipment, of course, can be dangerous as well as expensive.

This chapter explains first what equipment is necessary and what it will cost, and second how to maintain that equipment. The basic concept is simple: if you buy good-quality equipment and maintain it properly, you'll get many years of safe and efficient use.

A 1986-87 price list:

New light-duty western saddle ....$400–$600
New heavy-duty western saddle ....$600–$1,000+
Used western saddle.............................$300–$750
   English saddles similar in price and quality
Headstalls ....$15–$50
Bits ....$15–$50
Halters...$10–$20
Lead ropes ....$10–$20
Saddle pads ....$20–$40
Rain slicker...$35–$60
Hobbles ....$15–$30
Cotton foot rope, ¾" or larger ....$25+
All steel, tip-in rack for pickup ....$500+
New two-horse trailer ....$2,500+
Good used two-horse trailer ....$1,200+
Stripped four-horse bumper-pull trailer $3,500
Stripped four-horse goose-neck..................$4,000
Good used one-ton truck
   with stock rack ....$3,500+

A close-up of saddle tree construction shows the texture and almost translucent qualities of good rawhide shrunk tight around wood. —Hook's Saddlery

A craftsman shapes the groundseat of a saddle. This is the foundation of your comfort.

A quick inventory from the average ranges on this list shows nearly a $1,000 investment not including the price of a horse and horse transportation. Nor does that $1,000 include things in the nice-to-have category. All this expense is certainly worth careful treatment.

Western saddles

A sign in the post office warns about mail fraud in these words: "If it sounds too good to be true, it probably is." The same is true of western saddles. There are companies boasting roping-quality saddles for less than $300 while the average factory-made saddle of known quality begins at $600 or more. One wonders how the inexpensive saddle can be so inexpensive, since good construction takes two or more sides of leather at over $100 each, a tree at roughly $100, plus woolskin, hardware, stirrups, and many hours of skilled craftsmanship.

A western saddle's foundation can be checked easily. Lift up the seat jockey (the loosely curved piece that will lie under your thigh) and you can see the tree. If this is a heavy-duty saddle, that tree will be covered with smooth, hard, and somewhat trans-lucent bullhide sewn in tiny whip- stitches of the same material. If it is a light-duty saddle, the tree will be covered with

fiberglass fabric, or it may be of one-piece molded fiberglass construction. The latter will present a solid, smooth appearance similar to many plastic or fiberglass chairs, tool handles, etc., that we use daily.

Don't reject a saddle with a light-duty tree if other construction qualities are good. Those bullhide-covered trees are made for roping, and if you don't intend to rope, you really don't need that extra strength and weight. But do reject saddles with no tree covering, rough wood crafting, or a cloth-covered tree.

Now, pick up the saddle and hold it with the seat toward your chest. Give it a series of bear hugs and releases, alternating with a series of strong pulls in the opposite direction at the bottom edge of the skirts, as if you were trying to tear it apart. This tests for a broken tree. If you can feel weakness here—as if the tree were slightly hinged running lengthwise—this saddle has a broken tree, and it is essentially worthless. The only reason to consider it would be that the leather is all of good quality, and the price is down around the pocket-change level. In this case buy it, take it to the saddlemaker, and have him put in a new, top-quality tree. This will cost you $200 or more, but you'll still have made a good purchase. This broken-tree test is for used saddles and not something you need to do in a shop full of new saddles.

Next check for leather quality. Good
leather feels smooth and almost alive. It will
be of uniform thickness. Poor leather will be
coarse, particularly on its underside; it will
also feel dry, hard, and papery. It may be the
same thickness as good leather,
approximately three-sixteenths inch, but it
will lack uniformity of thickness.
Sometimes cheap saddles use belly-leather,
the lower-quality portion of a cowhide. This
will be extremely flexible and likely to
crinkle badly with any use.

Some saddles use two layers of leather
stitched together. This is acceptable if the
stitching is all good and if both layers feel
like good leather. However, if one layer is
paper-thin, if the stitching is worn out, if
layers are separated or missing in places, be
wary. These problems can be repaired, but
you shouldn't be paying much for the
saddle because you will be paying plenty to
the saddlemaker.

Inspect also for general construction
techniques. The best saddlers use nails to
hold leather pieces in place but use screws
for real strength. Some saddlers use staples
instead of nails, and staples should be
viewed with suspicion. They work their
way out easily; their crossbars may wear out
also, and the two remaining sharp ends will
stick up through some part of the saddle or
your anatomy. Check the stirrup leathers
and quick-change buckles. The best have
heavy leathers three inches wide and
sliding buckles (Blevins is a popular and
reliable brand name in stirrup buckles).
Cheaper styles will have narrower leathers
and tongue-style buckles, adequate for light

*Close-up view of a heavy-duty ¾ rig. Note that
the cinch will be pulling down from just behind
the fork (pommel). A full rig will be mounted
further forward, under the fork.*

riders but to be avoided for adults. A final
characteristic of good saddle construction
is the presence of long, strong saddle strings
front and back.

Be suspicious of efforts to cover
construction with fancy patterns, metal
trim, and unusual shapes. Tooled leather
can certainly be beautiful, but there are
degrees of quality in tooling. Strictly
speaking, tooling means a craft done
meticulously by hand with a variety of

The deep seat in this modified Association tree is similar to saddles from the early 1900s. Compare it to ...

... the flat cantle from sloping seat of the '50s. This one is harder to stay in, but comfortable as can be.

specialized tools. Some "tooling," however, is done by a machine stamp before the leather is put on the tree. This doesn't have the craftsman-like appearance, and it stretches almost flat as the leather is pulled into place during construction. Consider, too, that tooled leather is harder to keep clean because dirt and saddle soap will cake down into those tiny crevices. You'll be scrubbing with a toothbrush when you could be watching a football game.

Two other things you'll want to consider

are the rigging and the seat construction. Rigging refers to the apparatus used to hold the saddle to the horse. A full-double rig positions the front cinch as far forward as it can possibly be. This is mainly a roping arrangement, meant to be used at all times with a tight rear cinch. A full rig used improperly can sore a horse because it puts the cinch rings close to his moving elbow.

A buckaroo-special. Working cowboys who ride all day like the deep seat, slick fork. Beautifully built and comfortable. —Hook's Saddlery

An excellent choice for many people and many kinds of riding — an endurance saddle patterned after Army saddles of the last century. These are light, strong, secure. Note the deep seat. This model is handmade by Hook's Saddlery, Kalispell, Montana.

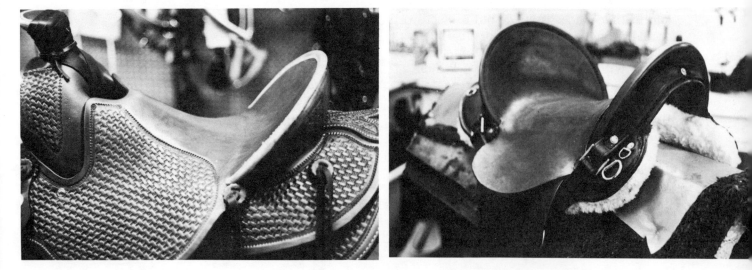

Also, it can pinch his withers if not used with the rear cinch, since it pulls the front end of the saddle down tight but leaves the rear up in the air. For general riding a ⅞ or a ¾ rig is better. These position the cinch further back so the problems just mentioned are no longer serious. For roping, however, the ¾ rig is less desirable because it allows the saddle to slide forward. A center-fire rig, which hangs the cinch still further back, is an anachronism to avoid.

Western saddle seats have come almost full circle in seventy-five years. Old-time pictures show high-backed seats with either a slick fork in front or a medium swell. Move up to the '50s and '60s and you'll find seats sloping back drastically, with flat cantles (backs). Now, in the '80s, the seats are flatter again, cantles higher, and forks available in considerable variety.

What's the difference? The high cantles and flatter seats let you sit forward on the horse, and they keep you down in the saddle more securely. They don't position your weight as well as English saddles, but they are better than the older sloping seats and flat cantles. Some of those older flat-cantle stock saddles, however, were as strong and comfortable as anything being made today, so don't turn up your nose at them. Just remember they were made for getting out of quickly in a calf-roping event rather than for keeping you on the horse.

Finally, whether you are buying a used saddle or just contemplating using one that's been in your family for a couple of generations, consider the overall condition. If the woolskin is worn away, the corners curled and dry, the stitching broken out, the stirrup-leathers cracked and hard, maybe you ought to just pitch it, or at least take it to a good saddlemaker for an estimate on a complete overhaul. Safety, your own comfort, and your horse's comfort all demand this kind of consideration.

English saddles

English saddles are also built for a variety of purposes and in a variety of qualities. Probably the most common and the most versatile are the jumping or all-around styles. Seats are relatively deep, and most have knee-rolls, either concealed or visible, sewn into the flaps for the rider's support.

Here again you don't want the cheapest. Poor leather and poor trees are problems just as with western saddles. Stick to the middle price ranges from reputable dealers, and you'll avoid the extremes of poor quality on one hand and pure hype on the other.

English saddles are measured differently than western saddles. A 15- or 15½-inch seat is standard for the cowboys, with a 16 being the large size. In English saddles 18

Details of English saddle showing the quick-release device used to mount the stirrup leathers. These two photos also come close to showing the texture and "feel" of good-quality leather whether on English or western tack.

inches is standard.

Other considerations are similar to those I've described for western saddles: leather quality, overall condition, tree strength, and particularly, condition of girth fasteners, known as billets. Also be sure stirrup leathers are hung from a quick-release device that actually works. This is a safety device that western saddles should have discovered by now, but haven't. If you fall, this device releases the stirrup leather from the saddle and keeps you from hanging up. I've been hung twice from the stirrup in western saddles, each time for only a few seconds. It's a heart-stopping experience that I'll cheerfully avoid any way I can. You can learn a great deal about English saddle construction by ordering a catalogue from Miller's. In addition to information intended to make you buy, this catalogue sometimes contains excellent discussions of tree materials and construction techniques. It also features a variety of brands ranging from the least to the most expensive, so you'll get a good exposure to prices and qualities.

Saddle care

If you don't want to replace your western saddle more often than necessary, give it the following minimal care. On one of those miserable winter days when you have nothing productive to do, bring your saddle in and let it warm thoroughly for several hours (by the way, all leather gear should be stored winter and summer where it will remain dry and out of the sunlight).

Scrub thoroughly with saddle soap or glycerin soap. Farnam's Leather New and a product called Lexol are both easy to use and very effective for this. Use the soap liberally, lather it well, rub it in with coarse rags or a sponge. Then wash it off with plenty of water. Pay particular attention to those areas that touch the horse—stirrup leathers and fenders—but also be careful in all areas that can collect dirt. Lift the seat jockey and scrub up as close to the tree as you can, also.

Let the saddle dry thoroughly, then oil it. Although there are many products available, the best is still good ol' pure neatsfoot oil. Avoid neatsfoot compounds. These don't do much good, and some leave an almost motor-oil texture. Rub oil liberally on the underside of each section of the saddle, and lightly on the outsides. Pull the stirrup leathers down a few inches so

The jumping saddle—practical, comfortable, versatile, an item which many western riders dismiss, but really ought to own. English saddles are excellent for schooling and using one is guaranteed to improve your seat.

you can reach in and oil the bend where the leather crimps around the tree. Remove the stirrups and oil the bent leathers where they hang. Really soak the undersides of the fenders since these get more horse sweat than any other parts. Unless the saddle has been hanging outside, you don't need to put more than a thin film on the seat. This will rub off on your clothes anyway. Don't oil padded seats. This cleaning and oiling process should include the tight spots between layers of stirrup leathers, and it should include the stirrups themselves if they are leather-covered. Finally, oil the saddle strings.

Once a year for this whole process is sufficient unless you ride in the rain a great deal, in which case two or three times will be necessary, particularly the oiling of outer parts. But don't get too carried away. Leather kept soft and oily all the time gets spongy and weak.

Neatsfoot oil opens leather pores and allows dirt to enter. It also dulls and darkens the leather. There is nothing you can do

about the darkening (it's harmless), but if you want to take the process one step further, get some saddle butter. This will let the leather shine, close the pores, and leave a nicer "feel." You do have to buff it. A good brand of saddle butter is available from the Ray Holes saddle shop in Grangeville, Idaho. Saddle butter can be applied to the saddle seat, although like neatsfoot oil, it will rub off on your clothes. It isn't quite as oily, however, so you won't mind it as much.

There are synthetic materials for these saddle cleaning jobs, but the products just mentioned most naturally complement the leather. Of course if you do want more protection on the saddle's seat without the product getting into your clothes, use the concentrated silicone sprays made for water-proofing boots.

The care I've described here is more than that necessary for English saddles. These can be cleaned more frequently (and easily) with saddle or glycerin soap and nothing else. Rub the soap in, don't flush it away, and buff with a soft cloth.

While you are cleaning your saddles, do your bridles and reins, too. The bent ends of reins and headstalls, at the point where they attach to the bits, are especially prone to rot since they collect a lot of the horse's slobber. Oil these more often than anything else.

Reins are prone to weaken where they touch the horse's neck, so this spot, too, needs plenty of oil.

A handy machine, though hard to find, is an old wringer washer. You can keep it out of sight behind the garage and use it several times a year to wash cinches, pads and blankets. Horse dirt and hair are too much for your household washing machine, and most laundromat owners will ask you to take your business elsewhere if they find you washing horse equipment. You can't really blame them.

When reins begin to show cracks or thin spots, replace them. The same is true of cinch latigoes, billets, or girth fasteners. Your life is on the line if these items break at the wrong time, so there is no excuse for keeping them when they show wear. Similarly, replace cinches when individual strands start breaking regularly, or when the whole cinch becomes narrow or stiffened.

Transportation

Whether you are buying a horse trailer or just looking yours over before the season begins, check the following items.

Stress cracks may show up as stretched paint, but more often will be a visible crack in a welded joint or next to a welding bead. These cracks are the beginning of the end. Get them re-welded and reinforced with additional metal welded across the stressed member. Consider replacing the member completely.

Wheel bearings are an inexpensive item, which can cause expensive problems if neglected. They should be free of stress cracks, flat spots, rust, or color changes. They are easy to check, easy to replace, easy to keep lubricated.

Trailer tires suffer the same stress as tires on the towing vehicle. They must be kept inflated, must have good tread, and must be rated heavy enough for your loads. It isn't safe to put your old tires on the trailer when you put new ones on the pickup.

Trailer floorboards are the subject of frequent horror stories. Keep them clean, and rap on them occasionally with a hammer. Good wood will rap right back while poor wood will absorb the hammer blow. If you suspect rot or poor quality lumber, replace the whole floor. Most floors are bolted down and not hard to remove. The bolts may be rusty, but a grinder will take them off and the floor can then be pried up. Replacement lumber should be 2-inch thick hardwood or the hardest of the softwoods, douglas fir or western larch. Leave drainage cracks between boards and the floor will last longer. A good way of preserving floorboards is to scrub them thoroughly, let them dry, and then soak them liberally with hot linseed oil. Smear this on with an old broom. Let it sit for a few days in warm weather and it will soak in well.

Miscellaneous maintenance includes running your hands along all interior surfaces to check for anything that could catch an eye or a piece of skin. Loose trim moldings, vents, and protruding latches are common culprits. Anything that could cause damage probably will. If the outer skin of the trailer is rattling or loose, use a pop-rivet kit to tighten it. This is work you can do without major expense and without a lot of specialized knowledge.

Stock racks are simpler to take care of than trailers, but they need the same kind of checking. Even though their construction is much simpler, they rattle loose from constant movement of the vehicle. Some wear can be avoided if you take the rack down and store it out of the weather when you aren't hauling horses. Be sure nothing along the front edges can catch halters or skin.

Coming home in a rain squall once, I didn't consider the comfort of the horse and, too late realized that even at only forty miles an hour rain stings badly when it splatters into your face. My horse figured it out faster than I did and crawled over the rack onto the top of my pickup cab in his efforts to escape. His front feet were smacking the window alongside my left ear and pounding hollows in the roof over my head. Always cool in a crisis, I slammed on the brakes and leaped out the passenger door into the road ditch. My next well-considered move was to jump onto the hood and beat the horse's face with my hat until he panicked and fell back into the rack. He tore a 4-inch gash in his armpit; the pickup and rack aged five years. Horses can do some amazingly stupid things, but so can their owners.

After this I attached a piece of reinforced plywood to the rack, taller than the rack itself. It not only solved the rain problem, but collected an amazing number of splattered bugs. Those too really smart at forty miles an hour. I've wondered since how that horse put up with his transportation troubles as well as he had up to this point.

Harness

Annually clean and inspect your entire harness. Barring accidents, a well-kept set will last through generations of driving. Since harnesses are all leather, treat them as you would your saddles, cleaning, oiling, and inspecting for weaknesses.

Cinches and girths

When of poor quality or poorly maintained these items can annoy your horse until he causes you trouble, or worse yet, can result in injury to you. What I've said about buying good quality is doubly true of the items that lash your saddle to your horse. There are so many good styles and materials available there is no reason to scrimp. A good roping-quality cinch, capable of withstanding years of hard use (I have one good one that is fourteen years old) sells for less than $25. Girths for your English saddle are in the same price range. For some reason novices often neglect this end of their gear, and you'll see ragged, filthy cinches holding down expensive saddles. Maybe because it's out of sight, it's out of mind. It shouldn't be.

Cinches can be cleaned several ways. One is to throw them in your wringer washer with the saddle blankets. This does a good job but is tough on cinches. Another is to stretch them on a board with a nail through each ring and scrub them with soap and soft brushes. Either way will keep them more comfortable for the horse and will help them last longer. While you're cleaning, make your safety inspection.

Unless you're roping, the rear cinch on ¾-rigged western saddles is pretty much excess baggage. On the full-double rig, however, it should be used at all times. This rear cinch, like other gear, should be strong and in good condition. It must always be attached to the front cinch with a short strap; if it isn't, it will slide back to become a flank-cinch, the item that encourages rodeo broncs to do their thing. The rear cinch must be kept snug against the horse's belly. Hung loosely, it has no function at all, except that it may tickle a jumpy horse and set him off. Worse, he can kick at a fly and hang a hind foot. You can imagine the rest.

Halters, headstalls, and bits

These are small, simple items that don't give much trouble. But some precautions are still called for, particularly with halters, since a poor piece of gear can lead to large frustrations.

The strongest halters are the flat nylon web halters. Stockman's is a good brand, though there are many double or triple strength, with large, heavy buckles. Avoid single strength halters with thin, sharp buckles, since these will break easily, and when they do, those buckles can cut. Some good halters close with a heavy snap, which is convenient, but I've had those snaps twist apart under strain, and when they break,

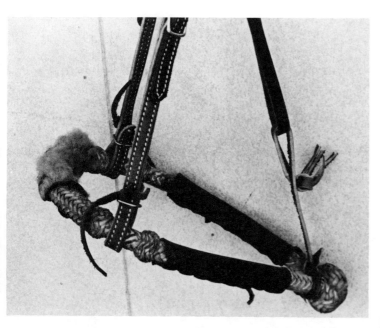

The bosal, or nosepiece of a hackamore: This one is wrapped to prevent chafing. Useful for training, though a true hackamore reinsman won't have this one with its standard headstall and cable core. He'll use a more complex headgear.

they can cut too. A good buckle is best even though it takes a few more seconds to use.

Good leather halters are almost as strong and considerably more attractive than nylon. Their only disadvantage is that they require more care than nylon does. Treat them as you do all leather gear.

Rope halters are a third possibility and the least expensive. The standard brand names such as Johnson's are strong and will last for years. Rope halters aren't very attractive, however, and they stretch and become likely to snag on fences, trees, and other protruding objects. But if you're careful and never leave them on the horse, they will serve well. Never leave a halter on a horse when you turn him loose.

The term headstall refers to everything on your bridle except the bit and reins. Headstalls are most commonly made of leather and should receive the same care as other leather gear. The same quality considerations apply too. But there are many strong, colorful, and easily cleaned synthetic materials now being used, and these, too, can do the job nicely. If you do use nylon headstalls, remember that sunlight will weaken them after a time; they should be kept inside when not in use.

A variety of headstalls are available in both English and western styles, with no one having any real advantages over others.

Mechanical hackamore: Not to be confused with the real thing. Also **not** to be used for training. Mechanical hackamores are okay for trail rides and are popular with ropers.

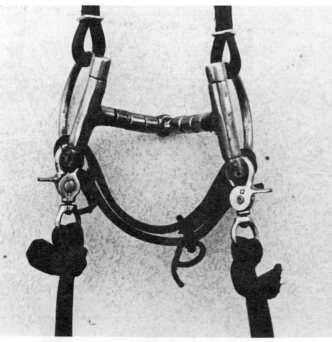

This snaffle has alternating copper and stainless steel rollers on the mouthpiece. A nice idea, but it does nothing that other snaffles cannot do. All snaffles depend upon direct pulling of the corners of the mouth.

Curbs (one with copper roller and one without) are more severe than snaffles. They are the standard bit for most uses on well-broke horses. The bump (port) in the center of the mouthpiece provides relief for the tongue when leverage is applied.

Though nosebands are not essential, it is a good idea to have at least one headstall with a leather noseband, since it can serve as a light and humane noseband for a tie-down. Cable or wire nosebands don't cure head-throwing any better than softer materials. They just hurt the horse more.

The English term for tie-down is a standing martingale. The English running martingale is the western training fork. Nylon models cost just a few dollars. Both types of martingales have their uses, and you will want one of each eventually.

As with other gear, there is a wide variety of good gear you can put between your horse and your saddle. Pads are better than single blankets for the obvious reason that they provide more padding. However, cheap pads made of foam rubber will squash flat in a few months and are extremely hot on the horse's back. Whether for English or western saddles, buy good pads of the now commonly used, washable, hospital fleece. The old standby wool is good, too. A good combination is to place a light wool blanket on the horse's back and a good quality pad on top of the blanket. The blanket is more easily washable; the wool wicks sweat away from the skin.

Some riders will use up to 2 inches of padding. This may be necessary in some cases but generally isn't a good idea. Too much padding moves the rider higher off the horse and makes the load more top-heavy than necessary. Also, too much padding makes the horse rounder, and you'll have to cinch extra tight to keep the saddle from rolling. Pad the horse, but don't overdo it.

Pads and blankets of unspecified, reprocessed fibers should be avoided because of what you can't know about them. Such pads could contain fiberglass or ground sawdust and may be extremely hot if nothing else. They may also shift and build odd lumps under the saddle.

When it comes to the bits, I suggest you read a great deal more than this book and rely more on your reading than on what you hear from neighboring horsemen. Bits are a technical tool that can be easily abused. The technology of their use has yet to penetrate

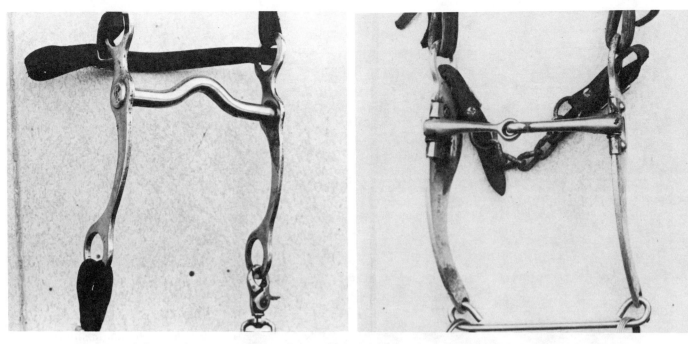

Curbs work by applying pressure to the tooth-free area on the lower jaw known as the bars and just behind the horse's chin where the curb strap lies. The bit on the right is a shanked snaffle.

the brains of many otherwise knowledgeable horsemen. The basic misconception seems to be that a bit is for "holdin' 'em" when it should be for "talkin' to 'em."

If you someday start a green colt, you will want a hackamore (bosal type, not a mechanical hackamore) or an English caveson for the first driving and riding lessons. This will save wear on your young horse's mouth. Once the colt is ridable, however, you will want to switch to the snaffle bit. Long-term use of the hackamore is a noble endeavor in the tradition of the Spanish cattleman, but it isn't particularly popular or practical for most of us. We aren't patient enough.

Snaffle bits are the mild training bits used in both western and English riding. Buy a good one, preferably with a solid copper mouthpiece not too thick. If you learn to handle the snaffle carefully and well, it alone, or with a running martingale, will be your main schooling bit for anything you do in the arena, even with your mature horse.

Curb bits can be confusing since many things, including the thickness of a horse's tongue, affect the bit's severity. But shank length both above and below the mouthpiece is your most obvious clue to severity. The longer that length, the more severe the bit, since more leverage is available to your hands. This is also true of shanked snaffles,

which are often misconstrued as mild bits. Anything with shanks operates as a curb, applying constricting force to the tongue, the tender bars (gums) of the lower jaw and the jaw bones. For a well-broke horse you shouldn't need more than 4 or 5 inches of shank below the mouthpiece, 2 or 2½ above.

Popular horse lore holds that copper mouthpieces promote salivation which translates to comfort, which translates to better communication. This doesn't mean that copper is the only good material for mouthpieces, however. Stainless steel is fine, and the old-fashioned sweet iron, which rusts all the time, is good too. Horses don't seem to mind the rust. It is we humans with our aesthetic sense who don't like the non-shiny products. Avoid cheap bits plated with a chrome-like substance. That substance will flake away and expose whatever poor quality metal is beneath.

If you get serious about training, you may purchase a full bridle, also known as a Weymouth bridle or double bridle. This consists of a headstall that accommodates two bits, a thin snaffle (bridoon) and a curb. Both will be in the mouth at the same time. This outfit will cost you $75 or more. It is an expert's tool and will, if used properly, give expert's results. Other bits such as pelhams or double-duty snaffles have single mouthpieces but rings for two sets of reins,

one in the snaffle position, one in the curb. Again, these are for training when you know the theory behind the practice.

The only care necessary for bits is to clean them occasionally of accumulated, caked slobber and chewed hay. Cleaning is also a good idea when you change from one horse to another. Horse diseases are often transmitted by oral and nasal discharge, so cleaning bits is an obvious precaution.

Miscellaneous

Skim this chapter's subtitles, and you'll see that the list of necessary gear isn't long, though it will cost plenty. A few more items will round out your general needs, though specific events, of course, will often require more gear.

Once you learn to use hobbles, you won't want to be without them. I'll mention types and uses in another chapter. A 20-foot cotton footrope is also handy for many things, as is a longe-line or two, and finally some good rain wear.

Be patient about gathering your gear. Shopping around can teach you what to look for, and it can save you money.

Perhaps your backyard horse outfit will never be thirty acres of white fence, irrigated lawns, and river view backed up against a few hundred thousand acres of mountainside. However, pride in what you do have will be necessary, as will a steady building and maintenance program.

chapter four
Doing Your Homework

Building fences, shelters, and pens before you bring home a horse may seem like common sense to you, but if so, I think you are in the minority. I've seen horses picketed by the neck in a weedy lot for a whole summer while the owner wondered about a more permanent place to keep him. Some people I know put a half-wild mare and her foal in a temporary pen at the edge of a few hundred square miles of mountains. The mare and colt broke out for a month-long frolic and were finally captured when they ran out of water. I once hauled two young horses a hundred miles to my uncle's farm for summer use by my cousins. Overnight the two colts walked out of a poor fence and headed home. It took us days to track them down; we finally dug them out of a hayfield forty miles from where they started.

Lack of preparation is another of these perception problems this book began with. Our perception or preconception of horsemanship often doesn't extend to mundane things like fences. But reality closes in fast when the horse arrives, and

you'll discover that having the mundane details attended to is what makes enjoyable ownership possible. I've divided these details into time, feed, space, shelter, transportation, and miscellaneous. None should be overlooked.

Time

Before you buy, you need to objectively assess the amount of time you'll spend on horses; for most of us, there just isn't enough. If you already feel your schedule is too crowded, you're kidding yourself if you think horses can be fitted in. It takes time to feed them, haul hay, clean equipment, keep your place clean, mend fences, and so on. These are the easy things, though not necessarily the fun ones. A half-hour ride will use up at least an hour since you need to catch your horse, clean him, saddle and bridle him, warm him up, all before you can do much real training or exercising. After the ride you need to cool the horse a little, put up the equipment.... And a half-hour ride isn't really enough to do much good, though it will be enough for some training sessions. To keep a young horse learning or a finished horse working well, you'll need several rides per week of an hour or more.

Most people in the northern states don't ride much from November through February, so there is no reason to count those dark months, but for the rest of the year you'll need to be religious about devoting time to your horses. Can you do it?

Feed

Having food on hand for your horse seems elementary, yet I continually hear from people seeking desperately for a few bales of hay to carry them a few days more. You need to ask yourself where you'll find a steady supply of hay and grain, how much storage room you need, and whether feed is easily available at all times. Picketing at the garden's edge and scrounging a few bales from the neighbor's haystack simply aren't adequate practices.

You must also have a constant supply of clean water. In hot weather horses will want water two or more times a day, and will consume five or more gallons each time. If you want to build muscles, (on you, not the horse), just pack water to them in buckets. But remember that you'll be packing that water several trips per day every day all year

long. If you go away, can you con your friends and neighbors into doing the job?

Install a water tank and hydrant for horses before your horse comes home, or run your fences down to the creek. You'll save a lot of grief. In some areas, though, land-use regulations may prohibit livestock in creeks or ponds.

Space

Horses like room to roam. That's one of the things we like so much about them. Unfortunately, backyard horsemen can't afford ten square miles for each animal, and besides, catching horses in big spaces is a little annoying. Something less will have to do, but how much less is open to argument.

Let's start with the one-acre plot. With one acre, you can keep one or two horses, but you aren't doing them any favors. They'll feel so confined they'll chew anything that doesn't hurt their teeth, and they may become grumpy too. But it can be done. After all, being out on one acre isn't nearly as crowded as being in a stall year-round, and that too is endured by many horses.

The one thing that makes cramped quarters bearable is regular exercise, but too often horses that have been standing still for months are suddenly dragged out for a spur-of-the-moment, all-day trail ride. Of

Sample plan for one acre, approximately 200' x 200'

```
100' x 100' lot for
house and garage

                                    75' x 150' arena


- - - - - - - - - - - - - -



100' x 100' lot for
pasture, miscellaneous



                              shelter and        30' x 30'
                              storage             corral
```

This arrangement provides space enough for two horses who get regular exercise and frequent changes of scenery. The horses' favorite stamping grounds will be near feed and shelter. This will also be where flies and manure collect. Thus, horses and house should be kept as separate as possible. The small pasture is a token only. It will not support a horse, but if well cared-for, it could feed two over a long weekend once or twice a month.

course the horse's manners and muscles are in poor shape. Most horses survive this kind of thing but not because "the exercise is good for them." Such exercise does nothing good for either health or boredom.

On two acres, things improve a little. This is still a two-horse space, however. On two acres there is room for buildings, an arena and a small pasture, room enough to provide a little variety, and room for horses to romp when they feel like it. It isn't enough space to pasture them, and it isn't enough to satisfy their inborn love of freedom. If you doubt me, turn them out in a big field some time after they've been confined in a small pasture, and watch them play. They know when the barriers have been moved back, and they like it.

One thing you can do to give your backyard horses some space is to rent a bigger pasture for the winter months. Plenty of farmers and ranchers will turn your horses out for a fee. While this gives your horses a good change of scenery, you have to watch their physical condition carefully. Sometimes so-called winter pasture has already been used for summer grazing, and there may not be much left. Also, if your horses are turned out with unfamiliar horses there will be some running battles until they clarify the pecking order. If your horse is injured in these battles, don't blame the landowner. He has nothing to do with herd instincts.

A five-acre plot is ample space for two or three horses. It has room for pens, corrals, and shelter, and if the pasture is good quality, it can support a few horses for a couple of months at least, especially if you keep them off the grass during the day.

Keeping your horses off the pasture during the day has so many advantages you'll want to do it even if you have an abundance of pasture. It keeps them from getting too fat. It makes them easy to catch when you want them. It makes them do their fly-stamping in the same spot all the time rather than killing off new patches of grass. It accustoms them to being locked up when you wish to be gone for a few days. Plots of land bigger than five acres begin to have possibilities for pasture rotation or hay crops in addition to the other facilities I've mentioned. Owning twenty acres, however, doesn't mean you have room for twenty horses. It means you can take better care of your land.

I've mentioned pens, corrals, and pastures as three separate items, and I want to clarify that distinction. By *corral* I mean a small (35 to 50 feet in diameter), high (at least 66 inches), and strong enclosure, square or round. It is an absolute must for horse owning. Corrals are where you lure the horse to catch him. Once you do this, you won't be teaching him little games where he lets you chase him around for a half day. Corrals are where you lock him up

Sample plan for two acres

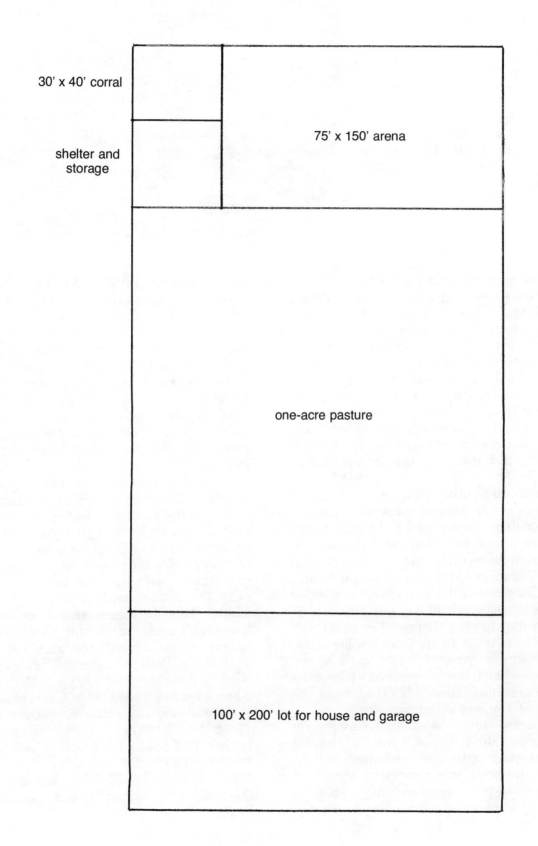

30' x 40' corral

shelter and storage

75' x 150' arena

one-acre pasture

100' x 200' lot for house and garage

Two views of an excellent corral built of railroad ties and rough-sawn planks.

for vet work. Corrals are where you introduce anything new and spooky during training. Corrals are where you put new horses until they get accustomed to you and your place. Corrals are where you separate new horses from old ones to avoid the worst of the pecking-order battles.

By *pens* I simply mean large corrals. Pens are less training places than holding places. They may be almost any size depending upon the amount of space you have, the number of horses, and the arrangement of your buildings. Keep in mind that horses penned too tightly will fight over feed or just out of cantankerousness, so pens for two or three horses need to be big enough for one or two horses to avoid the meaner one, something on the order of 30 feet by 60 feet. You may see fifty horses jammed into a pen this size on a dude ranch, but remember those horses work all day every day, and when they get the chance, they usually stand quietly. Even so, there are horse fights, and they can be a real melee as any wrangler can tell you. Pens don't have to be quite as stout as corrals, but they should be the best you can afford.

An arena is also a must. It can vary greatly in size and strength, and if you don't intend it for roping cattle, it can be made of light poles and posts. It is a necessity because it gives room to do some training without hauling somewhere every time you want to ride. A minimum size is 75 feet by 150 feet. This gives enough room to work at a slow lope, though hard running is out. It is also big enough for light exercise. About a dozen trips around its perimeter will equal a mile, and an hour of walking, trotting, and loping in here will be worth your time and your horse's. If you're short of space, build an arena anyway, and it will double as a main holding pen. If possible, an arena surface should be kept disked to a depth of 2 or 3 inches.

Corral construction should be of posts 6 inches in diameter or more, set at least 30 inches in the ground, 8 feet apart. Good railroad ties make the best corral posts. Corral rails should be of 2 x 6-inch lumber or heavy poles set close enough together that a horse can't stick his head between rails. The bottom rail should be high enough from the ground that a downed horse can't wedge a leg underneath. Four rails is a minimum with the top rail at least 5½ feet high. Rails all go on the inside of the posts so that riders don't hang up their legs when a horse gets too close. Gates must be as tall and as strong as the rest of the corral. There should be no wire, protruding gate latches, nail heads, bolts, etc. A nail head jutting out a quarter-inch can rip open a horse's face or shoulder deep enough to cripple him for the summer and scar him for life.

It's five and a half feet high, and with good gates will hold all kinds of trouble.

Though pen and arena fences don't need to be as stout as corrals, nor quite as high, remember that a nervous horse can scramble over a 5-foot fence even if he is a lousy jumper. Here too be sure that nothing protrudes. Never use barbed wire in your arena or pens.

Ideally you want to get rid of all barbed wire on your place. Horses and barbed wire go together about as well as babies and broken glass. Blood is inevitable.

Electric fence works very well with horses. Good electric fence should be of smooth #12 wire on posts twelve to fifteen feet apart, three strands or four, with the insulators preferably on the outside of the posts so horses can't snag themselves. Only the top and bottom wires need to be charged to keep horses from leaning over or reaching under. You don't have to keep the charger running at all times. While horses will periodically test the wire and quickly become disrespectful if they don't get zapped, most learn to leave electric wire alone for months at a time. A few, like an old mare we had when I was a kid, get so suspicious they refuse to cross places where there once was wire. I think they suspect some kind of a dirty trick.

Even if you keep a few cows, electric fence with heavy gauge wire is an improvement over barbed wire. Cows are far less respectful of fences than horses.

They will sometimes use barbed wire to scratch on, and they will crawl through any number of wires when they feel the urge to annoy you. Since barbs don't stop the cows anyway, use the electric fence, and you'll be far less apt to have fence injuries among your horses.

If you don't want wire fence at all, good rail fences are aesthetically pleasing and quite functional. But rails spanning more than 10 feet will sag in a couple of years, and round poles have a habit of rolling off their posts. Round poles also hold just enough moisture on their top sides to rot quickly. But, they are relatively cheap in some areas and easy to replace.

Planks 2 or more inches thick are better but far more expensive. In some areas planks can be purchased in the rough, and not only are these cheaper, they're stronger. Painting rough lumber is a miserable, paint-consuming task, however, and probably not worth the effort. Instead, stain rough lumber with a waterproof stain or Penta, a wood preservative. Using a sprayer makes the job much easier. This makes a durable and eye-pleasing fence. Smooth lumber (finished dimension lumber) is less strong but much easier to paint or stain. Never spend a dime on 1-inch lumber. Horses will break it down simply by leaning on it.

Plan for a two-strand electric gate

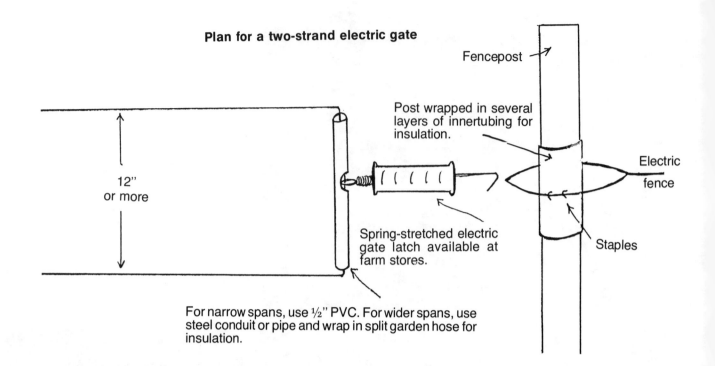

Fencepost

Post wrapped in several layers of innertubing for insulation.

Electric fence

12" or more

Spring-stretched electric gate latch available at farm stores.

Staples

For narrow spans, use ½" PVC. For wider spans, use steel conduit or pipe and wrap in split garden hose for insulation.

Building good fences takes some thought and effort. If you are going to the trouble of putting posts in the ground, you may as well make them big enough and deep enough to last. I once lived in a house that had nice white board fences around it, but the posts were untreated and set only a foot into the ground. One March evening a brisk wind blew most of this fence over. Rotted posts had weakened it, and those still sound weren't deep enough to stand the strain.

Your fences should be straight too. Run a string along your fence lines and dig holes along the string. Stretch wires tight. Use the straightest poles available in your area. Don't use steel posts with horses—they are easily pushed over by scratching fannies and then are useless and dangerous. A playful horse can run a steel post through his guts.

Gates are like the weak link in a chain. No amount of strength built into corrals and pens is of any value if your gates are weak. There is a wide variety of gate, hanger, and latch possibilities much greater than I can cover here. If you choose to buy commercially made steel gates, don't be shy about shopping around for price and quality, and remember you need to avoid anything that could catch an eye, shoulder, hoof, or rider's knee. It takes some thinking.

One kind of gate you can build inexpensively is illustrated here along with several types of inexpensive hangers. Latches? Pipe, chain, heavy hasps, you name it, all are used. Again, I illustrate just a few.

In planning the layout of your horse facilities, you will also need to think about where you will store your tack, stack your hay out of the weather, park your trailer or truck, dispose of manure, and store grain. Just as important, you must analyze the space you need for riding. This is especially true where kids are concerned since they will become tired of riding in a hurry if there is no variety. If your plans include a particular kind of competition or training, you will need very little space. Your arena will be adequate for dressage, jumping, pleasure-class work, and basic training. You can haul to other arenas for similar work. But if you want cross-country riding, think seriously about where you will ride. If you have to load up and fight traffic for an hour to get to open land for an hour or two of riding, chances are you won't do it very often once the newness is gone. This same is true if you board your horses out and have to fight the traffic to get to them. If you can only ride in one direction from your home, and that down a fenced gravel lane with

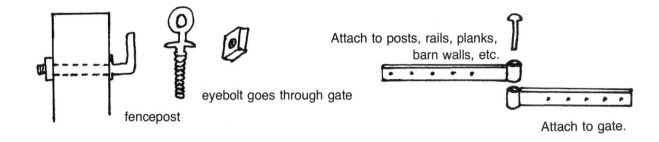

fencepost

eyebolt goes through gate

Attach to posts, rails, planks, barn walls, etc.

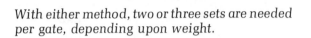

Attach to gate.

Two common gate hinges: these can be made at home if you're handy with a welder, or they can be purchased at hardware stores in similar patterns.

With either method, two or three sets are needed per gate, depending upon weight.

A short gate made of cull, dimension lumber, bolted together and painted with preservative. The pipe latch is simple and handy, but not as strong as the latch shown above.

Details of sliding 2" x 6" gate latch, very strong and handy. See drawings.

Detail of gate hanger—a piece of pipe dropped through a hole in top rail and down into gate. See drawings.

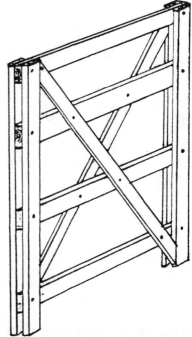

traffic whizzing at you from both directions, you soon won't ride much. If your kids can only ride around the nearest two blocks before they get into trouble with freeways, railroads, or city traffic, you are taking unwarranted risks, and you probably shouldn't be buying horses. And if there is open ground enough to please you, but it is all privately owned, you'd better talk nicely to the owner before you invest in horses. You could be all dressed up with no place to go if that owner doesn't like hoofprints.

A strong, easily-built gate, using the cheapest grade of 2" x 4" lumber. The gate plan can be altered to fit needed dimensions. Four rails are a minimum; five or six are needed for gates over five feet tall. Tack it together with light nails when building. Then bolt it together and pull out any loose nails. Countersink bolt projections so they don't injure horses or humans.

Detail of gate latching method

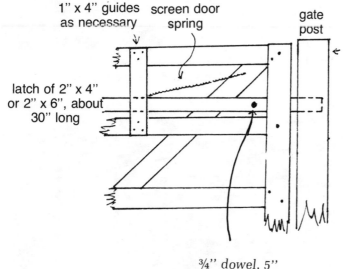

1" x 4" guides as necessary

screen door spring

gate post

latch of 2" x 4" or 2" x 6", about 30" long

¾" dowel, 5" long, as handle

p37

One good method of hanging a four- or five-foot wide gate up to 6' tall

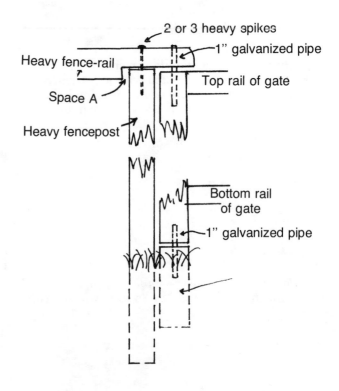

2 or 3 heavy spikes

1" galvanized pipe

Heavy fence-rail

Top rail of gate

Space A

Heavy fencepost

Bottom rail of gate

1" galvanized pipe

No sag gateposts

Space (c) will be filled with wire, plank, or poles, the same material as the rest of your fence. Though (b) can be nailed or bolted to the outside of posts, it is much stronger if inset. It should be a 2" plank or a heavy pole. Gate weight will pull down on the top of post (d), but (a) transfers the weight to (e) and (b) braces it

against the ground. (a) can be a plank lag-bolted on the side of the posts, hard #9 wire twisted between posts, or a heavy pole nailed to the top of posts. The same system can be enlarged at post (d) as much as you want for taller, heavier gates.

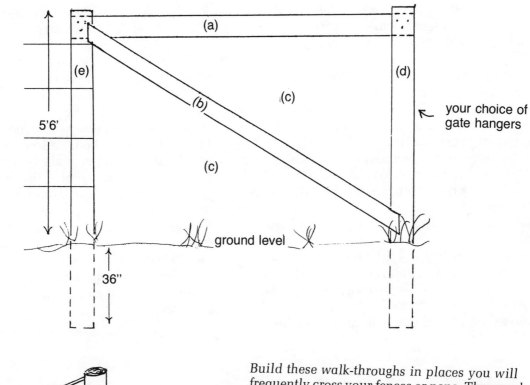

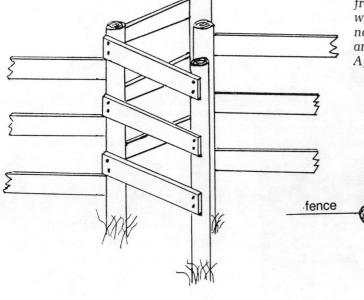

Build these walk-throughs in places you will frequently cross your fences or pens. They work with pipe, wire, plank, or pole fences. They are not a good idea in breaking corrals or training area since horses may bump into them at speed. Approximate dimensions below.

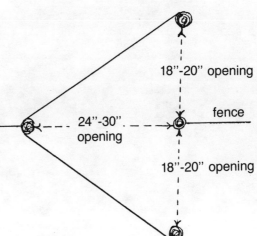

Shelter

Some owners like to keep their horses in an enclosed barn. In northern Minnesota we did that, tying four to six horses inside and packing water and feed to them for days on end while sub-zero temperatures and howling wind ruled outside. But even in that harsh environment, inside stabling probably wasn't necessary. What was necessary was protection from wind, cold rain, hot sun, and insects. All these can be had for considerably less expense than a complete barn entails.

Summer sun protection can be as simple as a good shade tree. Weeping willow will do the trick nicely, and a good one will grow big enough in seven or eight years. Lombardy poplars are also good if planted close together. For other uses and other seasons, something a little more elaborate is needed. A simple flat roof is a good beginning; so is a lean-to roof from a shed or garage. A roof will need to be 7 feet tall at its lowest point and cover about 10 feet by 10

feet per horse. This shade will keep flies down but won't slow mosquitoes.

A good stand of trees or bushes serves as a windbreak in summer or winter. In the wild, horses have survived a few million years using only such natural protections. You can easily improve on this with some simple carpentry. A wooden wall 6 or 7 feet tall is much better, and it can be made of the cheapest lumber.

Combine these two needs, roof and walls, in a three-sided shed, and you have excellent shelter, particularly if you build it with the long wall protecting from prevailing winds. It will be cool in summer, dry in winter, and open enough to allow timid horses to escape aggressive ones. You can extend the roof beyond the walls to get more shade. A 10-foot by 20-foot shed of this type will house two, three, or four horses, depending on how well they like each other.

A three-sided shed, eight feet by sixteen feet, its back to the prevailing wind. Room for three if they don't argue.

Slightly more complicated but even more practical is a series of 90-degree zig-zagged walls with a roof over the whole thing. This gives shelter from any wind and lets horses stay a little farther from each other. Such a structure, looking like the letter **W** when viewed from above, will be adequate for three or four horses.

With any shelter, a dirt floor is the most practical. Concrete is expensive, slippery, and hard on legs.

Whether you build shelter, shed, or barn, the considerations remain about the same: cost, space, wind protection, dryness, durability, and looks. Your horse won't worry about that last one, but you should, if for no other reason than the money you spend should be for something that enhances the value of your property.

Transportation

Not everyone needs a $5,000 horse trailer with bells and whistles, but sooner rather than later, every horse owner needs reliable horse transportation of some kind. Even if it hurts you to do so, you might as well add transportation to your list of things to study and buy before purchasing your horse, because nowadays, horse transportation is as essential as a saddle.

We'll begin from the premise that none of the super-light, compact, or foreign pickups are adequate for hauling horses. They may have the power, but they don't have the springs or the weight you need.

The bottom-line beginner's transportation is a full-sized half-ton pickup with a long-wide box. Ideally it also has heavy-duty springs. This vehicle will carry one horse with relative ease in a stock rack 5½ feet high. You can haul two horses in a half-ton pickup, though it isn't a good idea. Two horses are too much of a load to be safe on the highway, but for short, slow jaunts to the hills, you can get away with it.

Your pickup must have rubber mats or plywood, or both, on the floor, because metal floors don't afford a horse any traction. When he isn't falling, he'll be worrying about falling. (Discarded conveyor belting from heavy construction equipment makes excellent floor mats by the way, and sometimes you can get it free.)

Three-quarter ton pickups are much better for hauling two animals. These have bigger springs and shocks and give a much more stable ride. Of course, you can help the situation by adding heavier shocks with auxiliary springs, eight-ply tires in the rear, and over-load springs. Again, since the bed is identical to a half-ton pickup, you'll need plywood or matting on the floor. The cheaper chipboards will do fine, though they won't weather well.

If you haul one horse in a pickup rack, cross-tie him to help stabilize the ride a little. Hauling two horses is more stable since they don't waltz around as much, but it isn't as safe from the weight standpoint.

Hauling in pickups gives more maneuverability at less expense than a pickup-and-trailer combination. Horses will often load more easily into a pickup than into a dark, narrow trailer, and since a pickup is lower than a stock truck, you don't need much of a ramp to load from. In fact, most horses that load willingly will soon jump into your pickup from the road as long as they don't frighten themselves by slipping on the floor when they land.

While pickups have advantages over trailers, they also have disadvantages. First, horses make a top-heavy load, and you'll need to drive very carefully. Not only will they make you nervous weaving around up there behind you, but the fact that they are top-heavy makes horses nervous, too. Each bump and curve is exaggerated by the time the horses feel it. You'll need to accustom them to this ride carefully and with no errors, particularly on twisting roads. Once horses learn to ride, however, they stick like glue.

A related disadvantage is the business of stopping this juggernaut. You need top-notch brakes on your rig, but when you apply those brakes, the horses have nothing to brace themselves with except their noses against the front of the rack. You'll need to warn them that a stop is coming so they can sit back on their haunches a little. They'll learn this, too. A hard stop, however, is still out of the question unless you want horses wadded up in a panic-stricken pile in the front of your rack.

Another disadvantage, mentioned earlier, is that your horses will be exposed to the weather and to bugs splatting in their faces. A windbreak in front is the minimum you need to alleviate these problems, and you should have horse blankets for cold mornings.

A one-ton truck with 10- or 12-foot bed gives a stable ride for three horses standing abreast or up to five standing crosswise, head to tail. Beyond its size and stability, however, this outfit has the same problems as pickups. It isn't weatherproof, it certainly is no speed demon, and it requires cautious driving. In addition, one-tons and larger trucks require that you find a high ramp or bank for all loading and unloading. This is a real problem if you live in flat country. There you'll need a portable ramp, and nothing you can build that's strong enough will be light enough to handle without a lot of grunting.

Trailers come in such variety they may

confuse even the professional horseman, and the variety extends beyond style and type into quality. A flashy exterior on a trailer may disguise a flimsy interior.

Occasionally, someone has a homemade trailer to sell, or you may get the urge to build your own. Avoid both. Although *homemade* doesn't necessarily mean poor quality, building a quality trailer requires extensive knowledge of welding, of metal construction, and of just what trailers are supposed to do. Tandem axles mounted the least bit askew, for example, will peel your tires bare in a few hundred miles. A weak weld in a critical place can show up when your load of horses disappears over an embankment behind you.

Stick to commercially made trailers. Even then keep in mind that while most manufacturers are reputable, being *commercially made* doesn't necessarily mean top quality. You'll have to do some careful shopping.

A single-horse, single-axle trailer is the cheapest and easiest to pull, but it is not really safe and not particularly practical. If a tire blows out on a single-axle trailer, your number is up, so a tandem axle is much safer. And if you are spending money on a trailer, that trailer may as well have room for two horses, since neither the cost nor the weight will be much more. There are

trailers built to haul three horses abreast, but they aren't very popular because of the narrowness of their stalls.

In-line trailers, where horses stand single file instead of side-by-side, have the advantage of being easy to pull since their weight is independent of the towing vehicle. They are also handy in traffic because their narrowness allows the driver to easily view the road behind him. They are difficult to back and maneuver in close quarters, however, and some horses will not unload easily because the in-line design means they have to back an extra length.

Larger, bumper-pull trailers come as small as 5-by-14. These will haul four horses, but they will be crowded. If you are hauling four really large saddle horses, this crowding may cause a panic. A better minimum size is 5½ feet wide and 16 feet long, with at least 66 inches of headroom. By the time you work up to a 6½-by-18-footer, you can squeeze in five small-to-medium horses.

It's nice to have room for all those horses, but you're stretching your luck when you pull this load with a regular pickup. A minimum towing vehicle for a bumper-pull, four-horse trailer is a three-quarter ton pickup with a load-leveling hitch (load levelers are a good investment for any towing). I've pulled four horses hitched to the bumper of a three-quarter ton, but even though the trailer had its own brakes—an absolute must, by the way—I began to feel as if I were being followed by an unruly battleship. The major problem with this arrangement is the trailer outweighs the truck. A second problem is the bumper hitch places so much weight so far back that your pickup's front end, which is your control center, becomes too light for safe handling. A bumper hook-up by itself is inadequate for big trailers.

A better arrangement with bigger trailers is to tow them with a three-quarter or one-ton "dooly." This is still just a pickup, but it has the advantage of the extra stabilizing wheels.

With any of the large trailers, an improvement over the bumper hitch is the gooseneck. Here the trailer weight is concentrated on or just in front of the towing vehicle's rear axle. This is much more stable, maneuverable, and stoppable, and with this type of trailer the three-quarter-ton pickup is a safe towing vehicle. The gooseneck is obviously a variation on the tractor-trailer theme and it really works. It handles somewhat differently than a bumper-hitched trailer in tight places, and you'll have to get used to watching your mirrors, but overall a

gooseneck is an improvement over bumper-hitch trailers. Gooseneck trailers cost more, but they're worth the extra cost.

With any of the longer trailers, the 5-foot width has the same minor disadvantage as an in-line trailer: horses must back an extra length to get out, and they must back all the way out. Some don't like this. In trailers 6 feet and wider, however, horses can turn around and then step out. Also with trailers, 6-foot wide and wider, you can load and unload saddled animals without ripping apart your gear. In the 5-foot width, horses must go in naked.

Cost is a toss-up between trucks and trailers. Owning just a pickup or truck means less initial investment, but you will use a truck for more than just hauling horses, so it will wear out faster than a trailer. Trailers, for most people, are like horses: they stand home a lot more than they go down the road, so their cost may be hard to justify. If well cared-for, however, trailers will last ten, fifteen, or more years: amortized over that length of time, they aren't terribly expensive.

Your final consideration in buying transportation is to decide how many extras you want. You don't want junk, but it is a little foolish for a backyard owner of two horses to pull into a show with a six-horse trailer complete with dressing room, bar, and hot tub. The bigger, shinier, and more complex the equipment, the more there is to go wrong. Buy what you need, buy good quality, but don't confuse the size of your monthly payments with the quality of your horsemanship.

Miscellaneous

If you've accomplished all the planning and preparation suggested in this chapter, you are ready to buy your horse. Here are a few tips that will help him settle into his new home.

First, don't turn a horse loose in a new environment and expect him to be sensible about it. An old, well-broke horse might or might not be sensible, a young horse definitely won't be. Keep him penned for a few days, and you'll avoid trouble. This is just one more reason to have that corral built ahead of time.

Second, feed a light ration until he is comfortable with his surroundings and his new feed. Some horses can tolerate having their feed changed from thin grass to fat alfalfa without even a tummyache, but a good share do experience some gastric upset at much less change than that. A few will get colic from any feed changes.

Third, while he is penned, spend time with him. Don't jump on and ride immediately, but do catch him, brush him, handle his feet, longe him, and hand feed him. He'll develop a trust in you that will keep things calm on the first rides.

Despite the ungainly pose, this young quarter horse shows the muscle delineation that makes the breed famous. But he's untried and unbroke, a gamble for experienced horsemen, and probably a real dumb purchase for the novice.

Your first questions shouldn't be about breed or color, but "What can she do? How will she act? Is she sound?"

chapter five
Finally, Buying Your Horse

There are few good reasons for buying a young horse, and for the inexperienced rider, there isn't any good reason at all. The first principle to remember when you finally start looking for your horse is that you want a well-broke, mature horse. By well-broke I mean gentle, trustworthy, and well-trained.

You might well ask what would qualify you as an experienced rider. The criterion so many people use to judge their skills is the amount of riding done in childhood and adolescence. This criterion just isn't reliable. Most childhood riding, at least unsupervised childhood riding, can be discounted as experience in anything except hanging on and having fun. It definitely didn't prepare you for handling a young horse. In fact, it may have made you less able than an adult who is just starting, because it may have fostered the know-it-all attitude that becomes an obstacle to progress.

Here are some benchmarks that might help you appraise your experience. Even if you're convinced of your experience, check

anyway. Ask yourself these questions:

1. Have I had a series of lessons, perhaps twenty-five or more, on a variety of horses and for a variety of types of riding?

2. Or, have I spent a few years doing mounted ranch work on a variety of horses?

3. Or, have I been a horse show or rodeo contestant in a variety of events on a variety of horses?

If you can honestly answer "yes" to any of these, you might survive a young horse quite well; whether you progress beyond survival is another question. Notice the emphasis on a variety of horses. Being familiar with one horse doesn't qualify as experience with horses in general.

If you are a beginner, admit it, and go out looking for a well-broke horse of middle age. If you have done considerable riding but are still timid about horses, look for a well-broke horse of middle age. If you intend to begin a specific event—jumping, for example—buy a well-broke horse of middle age. Don't try to learn your skills on a mount that is too much for you. Young and green-broke horses are too much for many

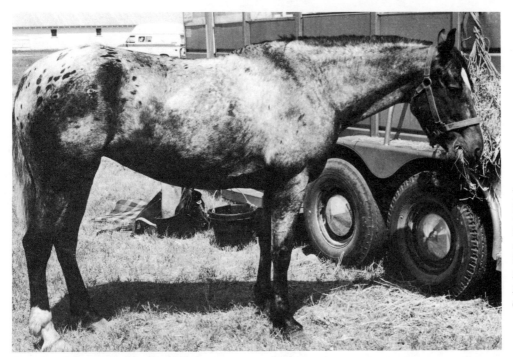

A nice looking light appy mare, maybe not halter-class quality, but tough, quiet, and dependable, an ideal backyard horse. This one relaxes after 35 mountainous miles in five and a half hours.

of their owners.

It may be cheaper to buy a young horse. But if the project dead-ends and you have to start over, or if you have to pay a professional to rehabilitate your horse, where are your savings?

Buy a well-broken, mature horse.

The second principle in buying is that you need a plan and some goals for the horse and for yourself.

Simply owning a horse is not satisfying for very long. Nor will ownership by itself bring you the results pictured in breed and organizational literature. Horses progress only when their owners have plans and goals. Owners grow satisfied only when their horses begin to conform to their plans.

The third principle when buying a first horse is that you want to give all breeds a good chance, rather than starting out as a single-breed fanatic. I'll try to explain what happens when this principle is ignored.

Walking horse and foxtrotter fans laugh about quarter horses "walking all day under the shade of the same tree." And while there is no doubt the quarter horse can't keep up to these other two breeds—he wasn't intended to—there are plenty of quarter horses that can maintain a smooth four miles per hour all day long.

Quarter horse people return the insult by lumping gaited horses together and dismissing them with the name

"stumblers." Yet gaited horses know where their feet are landing just as other horses do and are used successfully in the roughest terrain by open-minded owners. Quarter horse people also often dismiss Arabs as too dainty and flighty for "real work." Yet Arabs continually prove themselves in ranch work, endurance riding, and a variety of strenuous show events. Arabs have for centuries infused intelligence, stamina, and beauty into all other light breeds.

Modern cowboys almost exclusively reject Morgans, thoroughbreds, and appaloosas in favor of quarter horses. Yet Morgans were doing it all long before quarter horses were a recognizable breed. Thoroughbreds were the foundation stock for quarter horses. And appaloosas, despite a questionable start as a registry, have become serious contenders in many strenuous, athletic events.

The silly thinking continues when we assume that within a single breed, all breed characteristics breed true in all individuals. I'll use quarter horses again for an example, not because I dislike them—I own and use them—but because they are so visible and popular.

To those of us who fancy ourselves weekend cowboys, the general quarter horse characteristics—quiet disposition, big muscles, medium height, superior athletic ability—have become the standard by which we judge all other breeds. But to assume that a quarter horse is what all other horses should be, or to assume that all quarter horses fit our stereotype, shows ignorance. First, there are as many varieties of type and quality within the breed as there are within other breeds. There are vicious, hammerheaded, crooked-legged quarter horses. There are tall ones, thin ones, slow ones, ugly ones, dainty ones, crazy ones, you name it. Second, the older breeds—Morgans, thoroughbreds, Arabs—as I've already said, have contributed their genes to quarter horse success. Third, because of the numbers and availability of quarter horses, many are bred with no plan whatever in mind: the owner just wanted to "get a colt." I did this myself a few years back, breeding a top-notch Johnny Crier mare to an unpapered range stallion just because I thought it would be fun to raise a colt. Multiply that action by a few thousand each year, and you'll see why

there are so many kinds of quarter horses even in the line heading to the dog food market. In fact, as I write this the breed is in a crisis, and many serious breeders would like the dog food line to get more crowded so that prices and quality could improve.

This isn't to denigrate what the quarter horse is and does. The quarter horse is a fantastic breed, a success story Americans can be proud of. But when you're looking for a horse, you should list the qualities you need, then see if the individual fits your list. Don't ask if the breed fits, and don't try to fit yourself to the breed's stereotypes.

There is even more foolishness surrounding "breeds." There are people who will try to sell you a color-registered horse as if he had certain performance characteristics. The fact that a horse has papers declaring his coat to be yellow has nothing to do with soundness, disposition, training, stamina, or intelligence. The same problems arise with the half-registries. A

A tall Tennessee walker: a smooth ride and versatility, too. This breed is less common than many others among the backyard set, but ironically probably should be among the most common if its breed characteristics are considered.

A fine example of the Morgan type. The best of this breed compete in nearly any event, western or English.

horse born of a marriage of two different breeds doesn't magically inherit 100 percent of the stereotypical characteristics of each breed. He doesn't even inherit a 50-50 split of those characteristics. He does inherit approximately 75 percent of his dam's characteristics— disposition, size, abilities— and the rest comes from his sire. This half-breed horse will be an individual, not necessarily the inheritor of the best of two breeds.

That brings us to cross-bred, or grade horses. Are they worth looking at, or aren't they?

If you keep in mind that looking for a horse means looking for an individual to fit a list of needs, grade horses have many advantages for backyard horsemen, just as they do for many professionals. Grade horses are typically hundreds of dollars cheaper than registered horses, even if their capabilities are equal. A second advantage is that there are lots of them to choose from. Still another advantage is they aren't necessarily mongrels. Many grade horses are purebreds without registration papers. Others have one registered parent, and thus cannot be papered. Still others are intentional crosses by owners who knew quality but didn't care about paperwork. A grade horse's background may be as thoughtfully planned in many cases as that of some registered horses.

True, plenty of people will turn up their noses at your unpapered horses, but there are also people who would buy a three-legged giraffe if it were registered and would say your question about the neck just proved your lack of taste.

There are disadvantages to grade horses. One is that you cannot usually prove lineage for your own breeding purposes. Another is that any offspring will automatically be of lower value since they too are unregistered. Planning for offspring, however, should be done with some specific purposes in mind, so registered stock is usually better for this anyway. Still another disadvantage with grade horses is that shows and events organized strictly for a breed will be closed to you.

Many times grade horses are, nevertheless, your smartest choice despite their disadvantages, particularly if your goal is to improve your horsemanship. You can take an inexpensive horse as far as your capabilities will allow, then move on to another horse as many times as you like, without destroying your budget and normally without any less satisfaction than you would have from the average registered horse.

The fourth principle when buying is that you must become familiar with the standard list of horse characteristics all horse buyers consider.

Age

A two-year-old horse is old enough to break by gentle methods, but three is a better age because of further growing and strengthening. At four a horse can tolerate considerable work but is still too young for prolonged stress. At five he is mature, but for things like endurance riding seven or eight is a better age. By eighteen or twenty a horse is getting old. This doesn't mean he is finished, however. He may be slower, and he may stiffen up after hard use, but reasonable care will keep him useful for a long time. The last time I saw old Phoenix, she was a twenty-five-year-old dude horse, still charging high-headed to the front of the string all summer, still finding her own feed all winter.

Looking for a mature horse means that a fifteen-year-old may be a better buy than a five-year-old since the older horse will be so much wiser. You shouldn't, however, pay the same price. Sellers need to understand that when a horse reaches twelve, his value

may be decreasing, and after fifteen it definitely is decreasing. You should understand that buying a twelve-to-fifteen-year-old horse means you can expect from five to ten good years of use.

What about the risk of buying a fifteen-year-old and having him keel over at nineteen? No doubt that risk is there, but it is no greater than the risk of buying a yearling and hoping to get him to age five healthy, well-mannered, and sound: the chances of immediately enjoying the older horse are much higher.

A mature horse for adult buyers will be from five to twelve years old. For kids, keep in mind the saying: the younger the kid, the older the horse. If horses are broke and schooled at age three or four, they will usually have enough experience by five or six to make them trustworthy, providing they were honest horses in the first place. Be wary of the horse that was broke a long time past but hasn't been ridden for several

A lovely Arab that, along with its senior citizen rider, looks fresh and alert after more than 30 miles of trotting. This pair won the grand-championship in this tough, competitive trail ride.

This reliable little gray picks his way across a rockslide without a fuss. Two dead grouse and a shotgun hang from the saddle. He's been ridden clear up the mountain and back down with only a halter on his head, since his youthful rider forgot the bridle. He's not worth much on the market, but he's worth a fortune in terms of useability.

years. "He just needs a little tuning up" brushes over all kinds of idiocy in the horse world. Maybe he hasn't been ridden in all those years because when the owner did ride him, the horse was unmanageable.

Sellers have a habit of not remembering age very well. A good share of the horses advertised as nine, for example, are somewhere between seven and fourteen. Some advertised as fourteen are up to twenty. A rudimentary knowledge of judging a horse's age from his teeth will help save you from paying for years that have already passed.

In horses up to ten or twelve years of age, a sideview of the incisors shows them growing almost vertically. The older they get, the more horizontal they grow, as if the teeth wished to push out of the mouth. Also, at age ten a groove appears near the gum on the third incisor; over the next ten years it grows down the length of the tooth. In very old horses, teeth will be worn down short and aiming forward obliquely. This isn't hard to spot at all.

In young horses you can watch the temporary teeth fall out and the permanent ones take over. The center two, top and bottom, are replaced by late in the second year. The next tooth on each side is replaced by late in the third year, and the next two before age five. Any horse that has all twelve full-size front teeth has to be five or older.

You can learn even more specific aging with the teeth by reading the shape of the cutting surface. Many horse health books have pictures and diagrams explaining all the details of tooth aging.

Disposition

Disposition is the sum of personality, trained manners, and experience. In horses, as in humans, disposition can swing from delightful to unbearable within an individual, and consequently it is difficult to define. Disposition is also extremely important for you as a buyer to consider because, assuming the horse is healthy enough to use, disposition is the one characteristic of your horse that will determine whether or not you actually like him.

In chapter six, I discuss various dispositional types. Understanding these will take time and experience with many different horses. For the purposes of buying, there are three traits to consider. First, ask the seller bluntly how this horse gets along with other horses. Some horses love to fight and will hurt you, themselves, or another horse. At the least they will be troublesome to keep since they must be penned away from others. Second, don't be impressed by the romance of a snorting, high-headed, wild-eyed wonder that cavorts in huge circles around you and the owner. That looks great on those K-Mart paintings, but it isn't much fun to work with. Look for a quiet, alert disposition both when you're riding him and when you're working around him on the ground. Third, remember that it will take months before you have a clear picture of this horse's disposition, and that disposition will change gradually as the horse ages. Some horses sour with age while others outgrow a coltish, spoiled-kid act and become sweethearts. You can't blame the seller for hiding the subtler dispositional traits from you. They may take a long time to make themselves known.

Though large size can be useful in horses, for the backyard horseman it should be far down the list of priorities.

A horse is measured in "hands," an ancient term now standardized at 4 inches. Measurement is taken from the point of the withers to the ground. Any horse under 14 hands 2 inches (58 inches) is considered a pony, although anything from 14 hands up may be called a horse until careful measurements are taken. Weight and proportions figure into actual size too. Some short horses are so well-proportioned and powerfully built they don't appear small at all.

A 14-hand horse is considered quite small, while a 16-hand horse is tall, at least in western riding. In English riding, particularly in jumping events, 17-hand horses aren't uncommon. Within this 14 to 16 range your choice of size may have more to do with whether or not you split your jeans while mounting than it does with the horse's ability to carry weight. There are powerful and tough 14-hand horses, and there are weak 16-handers. Furthermore, the bigger a horse gets, the more he eats, generally, and the less efficient is his strength-to-weight ratio. Don't get hung up about this. The most efficient members of

Well-broke horses will put up with all kinds of things, including kids, dogs, and spring run-off.

the horse kingdom on the basis of strength are the hardy Shetlands and donkeys.

If you are over 6 feet tall you will want to avoid small horses as a matter of proportion while you are mounted. All things considered, it is silly to buy a little horse for a big man, but it is just as silly to put large size at the top of our priorities.

I once used an 800-pound Arab as a pack horse on an eighty-five mile trip. He carried only 15 pounds less than my other pack horse, an appy weighing nearly 1,200 pounds. I led both with a big, fast-walking horse that needed few rest stops, so there was little mercy shown on this trip. That little Arab did everything the big horses did, including climb mountains, wade rivers, and for a couple of days, travel on short rations. Surprisingly, it was the Arab that seemed to thrive on the hard work and that had plenty of energy left to cavort about when I turned the horses loose to graze at night.

Common sense tells us there are times when the more efficient small horse just isn't enough. But if a horse is easier to mount, lighter to shoe, cheaper to feed, and capable of all the work you want, his shortness is a minor item.

Discussing size leads to the question of which is best for kids—horses or ponies? Many factors other than size enter this calculation, but if you're considering a small pony—less than 13 hands 2 inches—here are some of the pros and cons. On the negative side:

- Small ponies can be troublesome because they are so smart, tough, and independent.
- Small ponies are rarely well trained. Adults are too heavy to train them, and training ponies is seldom profitable, so the job just doesn't get done.
- Your children will outgrow ponies faster than you can imagine.
- Small ponies can't usually keep up to big horses on long rides, though this is more a matter of walking speed than endurance.
- Small ponies have little resale value.

Pluses for ponies include:

- Despite what some people will tell you, small ponies are not necessarily mean. They can become favorite pets.
- Kids can bridle, saddle, and mount ponies without help.
- Ponies have few health problems except for those that come from overeating.

Medium and large ponies, those from 50 to 58 inches, are a different story. These can carry older kids or even lighter adult visitors to your home. Some can really walk,

Though the hooves on the gray are obviously bigger than those of the white-legged horse, the gray is smaller by four inches. The gray's legs are heavier, too. For the serious horseman, that means that the gray, though less picturesque, is the better bet to work hard and long without foot and leg problems.

while others will have the short, choppy gaits you'd expect from a short-legged animal. Almost all are tough, efficient, and hard-working.

Color

Color could be the subject of a book all by itself and in fact, is the subject of frequent magazine articles. But color, like size, should be low on your list of priorities. Color may have something to do with your initial impression of a horse and your pride in him. It may have something to do with resale value too. But most colors lose their importance if your animal can prove himself in performance.

Dark bays and sorrels are the most popular in several breeds. A dark gray will bring extra money in the sale ring as will a line-backed buckskin, at least with quarter horse fanciers. Palomino lovers have parlayed the obvious beauty of their favorite color into a breed registry, but remember such registration certifies only color, not performance (It is easy to get hooked on palominos. We had several when I was younger, one a flawless mare who gave us several palomino foals. Few of the foals, however, measured up to the mare in looks

or performance.) Pintos and paints—the latter refers to pintos of quarter horse ancestry—are also popular colors, and several competing registries offer papers that increase the value of your horse.

I saw a buckskin once that was only buckskin from the ribs back; his front half was black-and-white pinto. When color gets this exotic, you'll need a real sense of humor and impregnable self-assurance to bring him out in public. If there's a lesson here, it is probably that whatever the color, some uniformity is desirable.

Conformation

Deciding what color or size you'll accept is much easier than deciding what constitutes acceptable conformation. Conformation refers to build or physique. I'll describe the universals that can be useful no matter what breed you're looking at. Each breed association has its own interpretation of these characteristics, so you'll have to study breed literature and outstanding representatives of each breed to teach your eye what it needs to see. But with each breed there have been mistakes too, usually when breeders value looks for their own sake rather than as aspects of

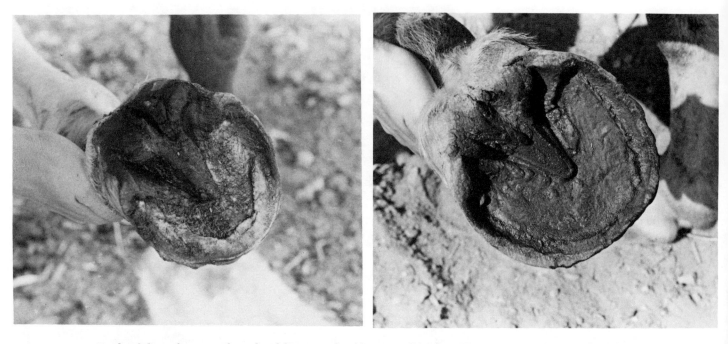

Both of these hooves show healthy growth of horn and frog. However, the right hoof (again from the little gray horse) is broader, with thicker horn and more growth under similar conditions. At any rate, the heavier hoof is superior in strength and longevity.

performance characteristics. When, for example, you become confused over what an Arab is really supposed to look like, fall back on the universals.

Start looking at horses from the bottom. Hooves should be solid, preferably black. Don't be charmed by tiny hooves and legs on a horse of any size. This combination can be a real weakness. It's a simple matter of pounds per square inch. Flat, splayed-out hooves may be acceptable, but a somewhat more tubular shape is preferable since these, like a mule's hooves, keep the hoof sole up off the ground. Hoof walls should be free of major cracks, those where the outer wall is actually split. A hoof left untrimmed for a long time may have short cracks that will break off during trimming. Since a hoof naturally trims itself by breaking off in small pieces, don't assume natural breakage is a flaw.

Pasterns, the short section of leg just above the hoof, should rest at approximately a 45-degree angle. If the horse is built so that his pastern is nearly vertical, he will be rough to ride and prone to navicular disease. If the pastern is weak, it will be nearly horizontal when the horse is standing. Some variation is acceptable, but either extreme is a flaw.

Look the legs over carefully. They should be free of wind-puffs, major scars, swellings, etc. If you look at a variety of sound legs, you will soon notice the occasional oddities fairly easily. While a horse can recover fully from some nasty lamenesses and injuries, the worst of these will show on the outside to a knowledgeable eye and should make you wary.

Splints are one exception to your need for wariness. These are round hard lumps about the diameter of a quarter a few inches below the knee on the front legs. Though they cause pain while forming, most do no harm once they have solidified.

Leg bones should be large and strong, knees large and flat. A horse's legs should stand straight under him without angling in or out. He shouldn't be pigeon-toed or splayed-out either. The hind legs when viewed from behind will usually be closer together at the hock than at the top or bottom; if this "cow-hocked" look gets extreme, it is a major weakness, not to mention an odd-looking arrangement.

A horse should have a sloping front shoulder and a sloping croup (from the top of the rump to the base of the tail). You can picture what happens when a vertical shoulder is combined with vertical pasterns. Jarring is greatly increased to both horse and rider.

The back should be roughly as long as the neck, and though some variation is acceptable, avoid a short-neck, long-back combination. Visual considerations aside, the proportion of neck to back can affect speed, balance, handling, and the ability to bear weight. Necks may seem unimportant to you until you own a horse with a short, heavy, naturally cresty neck. He will lack flexibility, and because of the power in that neck, may be inclined to put his head more where he wants it than where you do. Leave horses with short, thick necks for harness work.

For beauty fanatics, the head is a focal point, and many people want all horses' heads to look Arabian. This means a small head, wide between the eyes, dish-faced, with large eyes and tiny ears. There is no doubt about the beauty of the Arabian head—on an Arabian. But the look isn't desirable or even pleasing on horses built differently than Arabians. "The head is a

long way from the legs," old horsemen say, and consequently it doesn't much affect usefulness.

But if the head is way too big, or is badly Roman-nosed, or has tiny, pig-eyes, your pride will suffer, and there is some correlation between the shape and expression of the head, and a horse's personality and intelligence. Some horsemen say they can predict disposition accurately by looking at the head. I'm not that good, and I've seen some pretty heads on ugly customers. But the relationship is there in some degree.

You don't want to buy a pretty head attached to a worthless horse, but you don't want to discount the need for a reasonably attractive head either. Look for a head in proportion with the rest of the horse, a head with width, large eyes, proportionate ears, and no unsightly bumps or cavities.

The last item of good conformation is defined withers. Round withers force you to cinch down tight to keep the saddle on. This is uncomfortable for the horse and annoying or dangerous for you if the saddle rolls over.

Soundness

Soundness means having no skeletal, muscular, cardiovascular, or digestive weaknesses that might interfere with working ability. Soundness is equal in importance to disposition. If a horse is sound you can accept some conformation flaws in him, but if he isn't sound, the most perfect build and disposition don't mean much. An unsound horse normally shouldn't even be purchased for breeding purposes since the unsoundness may express genetic flaws, which could be passed on.

Though it may take months of use to know for sure if a horse is sound, there are simple tests to use before you buy. These will be good first indicators at least. Lead the horse at a walk and trot while watching for uneven bobbing of the head. A sound horse will bob his head little and in regular beats; a lame horse, particularly one lame on a foreleg or foot, will have a pronounced bob at one point in each stride. Another test is to pick up each leg and bend all joints up tight for perhaps sixty seconds, then drop the leg and move the horse out smartly. He should move freely and still bob evenly. A stiff start or uneven bobbing will indicate some joint lameness at least. Still another

test is to press sharply on the frog of the hoof with a blunt instrument such as a screwdriver handle or a pincer-like hoof tester. If the horse flinches, there's a good possibility of navicular disease, a serious and ultimately incurable problem.

A final check for lameness or potential lameness is to evaluate hoof quality. Poor hooves can often be rehabilitated with careful shoeing and the feeding of vitamin and mineral supplements, but if there are multiple, deep cracks or obvious deformities, avoid the horse.

Because some poor-looking feet are tough and some good-looking feet are tender, you should test for tender feet. This is easy if the horse is unshod. Lead the horse for a few minutes on a coarse-graveled road. If he immediately seems to be walking on eggs, he's likely to need continuous shoeing. This isn't as serious as some problems, though it can be annoying. Any horse will become sore-footed after a few miles on gravel, but a horse with reasonably tough feet will travel some distance before the soreness begins. Tender feet may not seem like much of a problem to you until you want to do some serious work. A sore-footed horse is as good as no horse at all, since he can think of nothing but those feet.

If you doubt your ability to perform these soundness checks, spend a few dollars to have the horse checked by a veterinarian. He'll not only check soundness, but all kinds of other general things as well and usually all for the one price. This is money spent well. Remember, however, that some vets specialize in horse care while others specialize in Pekinese dogs. They'll charge about the same price, and they both know their fields, but I think you know which one you want working for you.

Small traits, big problems

A horse that won't let you handle his feet is nearly useless if you live where shoeing is at all necessary; that encompasses much of the United States and Canada. I had a lovely appy mare once who was difficult to handle from the knees down. I spent hours persuading her gently that she was wrong. I failed; when she went through the sale ring that summer, she wore two front shoes tight, one rear shoe flopping from three nails, and a wealth of scars from bashing her head on stall walls and Mother Earth.

It is possible to throw and hogtie such a horse, and you should eventually learn how to do this. But throwing requires two people to accomplish safely, and it is always a rough situation. Your friends won't volunteer for this duty more than once, and

your shoer will charge combat pay for putting up with it. You can tranquilize the horse, but this too has its dangers.

A second little annoyance is the horse that's hard to catch. If I had to put a monetary value on personality traits, I'd say this one is worth ten percent of the purchase price. Few things are more frustrating, even in one acre, than chasing a horse that loves the game and reinforces his own understanding of the rules every time he succeeds at it, which is every time you go out after him. You in turn cannot punish him when you do catch him, because then he thinks he's being hammered for having stopped. For you, it's a no-win situation.

A third annoyance is the slow walk. While there is a wide speed range between the three-mile-per-hour hustle of a pony and the twelve-mile-per-hour poetry of the Tennessee walking horse, the average horse, working at walking, is in the three- or four-mile-per-hour category. Some never do learn to walk honestly. You need to kick and spur them along constantly. They lag back for a while and then trot to catch up, then lag back again. It is annoying and embarrassing.

If you intend your horse strictly for arena work, however, or for an event where walking speed is of no consequence, you may not mind a slow walker. This is just one small reason to have a plan for the horse before you buy. But if you want a cross-country pleasure horse, the best price, the prettiest color, the soundest feet will all sour if the horse cannot or will not walk.

Item four is what I call prancing and dancing. Symptoms include head-throwing, foot-slamming, a chin sucked tight against the chest, and traveling more sideways than forward. This may look romantic in a parade, but it will be miserably uncomfortable to ride for any length of time. It is also tough to get any response from this horse, because he has over flexed his neck making communication through the bit and reins impossible. The horse is "behind the bit." Though many horses begin each ride prancing, most settle down in a few minutes. If they don't settle down, avoid them.

Next is the puller, a horse who throws himself back against the halter rope. Some do this once or twice as colts and never do it again. Others do it their whole lives. Check this by startling the horse from the front while he is tied. A puller will throw himself back to the end of the rope, lean down into it, and, if it doesn't break, start shaking his head back and forth violently. If the rope still doesn't break, he'll eventually leap forward and stand again. If you're too close during the performance, you could end up in the hospital. A non-puller may jump around too, when you startle him, but he won't hover dangerously out on the end of a taut rope. There are gimmicks to help cure this problem, and I mention some in a later chapter, but in an older horse the habit may be permanently ingrained. You may learn to live with it, but you won't ever like it.

The last small item, which could be a big headache, is the general condition of the horse. If he is obese on light forage, he may be prone to grass founder. If he is skinny on good forage, he may require constant extra attention. Find out about these things if you can. If his attitude is listless, or his coat dull and patchy, or his skin suffering badly from flies, he could be getting poor care, but he could also have minor, but chronic, health problems. I once owned a gelding who had recurring ringworm. It never affected his usefulness, but it did require messy salves, and I didn't like the idea of having his problems on my skin. No big deal, but annoying, especially if it had spread to the other horses.

Beginning horsemen worry a great deal about their new horses bucking or kicking, and while these things are dangerous, they aren't nearly as common as the minor problems I've just mentioned. True kickers are so dangerous most people won't dare sell them to you. Even if you did end up with one, you'd be so scared of him that it wouldn't break your heart to get rid of him. A true bucker isn't likely to be sold to you as a broke horse since his bad habits are so easy to spot, and if you did end up with one, there is a good market for these on the rodeo circuit. But the six little items, though they may seem insignificant while you are buying, can exasperate you until you don't want to handle the horse. They are significant. Find out about them before you buy.

How do you go about finding a horse?

Start reading the want ads to check prices and available animals. Go to a sale barn and just watch for an entire auction. Visit a few dealers and breeders. Whatever you do, don't get in a panic to buy the first animal you see. Someone else may get him, but believe me, there are more horses out there, and good ones.

Finally, go ahead and buy.

From whom? I can't answer that. No matter what method you take in choosing a horse, you are gambling. Finding an owner who will guarantee his stock is a hedge against the risks, but you are still gambling. A breeder or dealer can be dishonest or ignorant or accidentally wrong. An individual owner presents the same possibilities. Sale-barn horses may be the worst culls in the world no matter what the auctioneer says about them.

But you can reduce the risks.

One way is to carefully explain to a professional horseman what you want, and then either have him find such an animal for you, or pay him to accompany you on your horse-hunting days. Remember to ask for a guarantee if you do buy, but remember the seller is taking a risk too. You could take his horse home for a week and ruin it. Be fair in your request.

You can substantially reduce the risks if the seller allows you to take the horse home on trial. A week's careful use will teach you more than all the talk in the world. Understand, however, that you will be responsible for damages to the horse.

If you buy through the sale barns, think of this method as simply taking a horse on trial. Promise yourself you will give the horse thirty days of good care and steady use. Then, if you don't like him, take him back to the sale barn and get rid of him. Will he go to the canners? Maybe. Maybe not. Will you break even financially? Maybe. Maybe not. But even if you lose a few

hundred dollars, you aren't pouring a winter's feed through an animal you hate, fear, or can't ride.

You can use professional help another way. Buy your horse, then pay a pro for several weeks of lessons for both you and the horse. Ride under that supervision until you develop a working relationship with your new horse. It will be expensive, but it will be money well spent in the long run. I told you this wasn't going to be a cheap hobby.

Finally, in your search, remember this last principle of horse-owning: you are never going to find the perfect horse.

Since horses are individuals, each has his own quirks. Some quirks you won't notice but other people will. Some quirks will drive you bananas. Part of horsemanship is learning to live with what you can't fix and at the same time learning to fix what you can't live with. That may simply mean you have to be more patient; it may mean you must learn some training or rehabilitating techniques; it may mean you must sell the animal. Don't curse the former owner for your horse's quirks unless it is immediately obvious he was dishonest. Part of the problem is likely to be you, not the horse or his background.

Don't give up on horses, either. The search for a perfect horse adds spice to ownership. If you learn to enjoy a horse, get the best out of him, learn from him, then move on to another, you have a lifetime of pleasure and anticipation ahead of you.

Half-wild range horses string out behind a wise gray mare.

chapter six
Horse Psychology

One of the reasons novices frequently have trouble with their horses is they don't understand horse psychology. Ask old-timers about horse psychology and most will laugh you right out of the corral, but there is such a thing, and many of those old-timers knew it well. They just didn't have a name for it. This chapter begins a study of the subject. You should begin to watch your horses carefully to see how this psychology works, and you should read a great deal more than this chapter. I'd suggest you start with Robert W. Miller's *Western Horse Behavior and Training.* Other books listed in the appendix will also be helpful.

Though I divide this discussion into two parts, herd psychology and individual personalities, in reality the two blend so subtly it is often hard to separate them.

Herd psychology

In the wild, horses don't feel secure very long without other horses in sight. The herding impulse is so tied to survival that it long ago became a part of the horse's genetic makeup.

Like other animals living in groups, horses develop a pecking order based upon dominance of each other and reproductive roles. This learned order becomes so ingrained that it operates within a herd with a minimum of signals. Horses learn to keep their places or suffer the consequences. A smart old mare chooses routes of travel and expects the first pick of available feed. There is no such thing as voluntary sharing. She may let others paw away the snow, then steal what they have uncovered. She has established her position with teeth and hooves, but most of the time she maintains it fairly calmly, with a flick of one ear, a quick swish of the tail, a feigned kick. The others on down the order will use the same signals to assert their positions. You'll see the same behavior being used by as few as two, old partner horses spending their days penned. About the only difference between your domestic herd and a wild one is your herd won't panic at the sight of humans, and a gelding may be boss. Your horse's habit of avoiding capture when you want him is a leftover of the wild herd's wariness.

Trouble occurs because horses never quite leave well enough alone. They often have an urge to better themselves, and they force the next horse up or down the hierarchy to defend himself. Consequently horses in a herd wear a lot of scars, despite the eons their ancestors spent living together in the same patterns. This is the reason you must be so careful about putting new horses together and giving even old friends enough room to keep away from each other. Mules are smarter about this than horses and less often hurt each other. They will, however, dominate and often hurt smaller animals such as calves, colts, dogs, or even children.

Trouble can also develop because some horses simply think it's fun to beat up on others. I have one that will stand like a kitten for hours, then without warning launch a full-scale attack on his buddy's ribs. I have never seen the buddy do anything to deserve this. Once the bruises are laid, things quiet down again until the next sneak attack.

When horses are closely confined as they will often be in a backyard operation, their herd instincts don't die, but they may be changed to some extent by the circumstances. I'm convinced that single horses or small bunches of up to four, even if handled frequently, fit their handler into their pecking order, though their understanding of the relationship may be a little naive. In other words, each horse, rather than figuring out how to fit himself into your plans, figures out how he fits into the herd order with you as part of the herd. If he is handled with calm assertiveness, he submits to your needs because he accepts you as the boss hoss. If you are too timid around him, he sees it as a chance to move up the ladder, and he gets hard to handle.

A pack horse, owned by an outfitter, who's a friend of mine, has to be chased into a corral and roped by a good roper. But once he's roped he folds his bluff. I once shod him without tying him up—just dropped the lariat tail on the ground out in the yard and went to work. I don't know how the horse came to have these peculiarities, but I do know they were his interpretation of what he should do within his herd.

Herd psychology appears in individual horses in several ways, the first being simply the need for company. Some will go crazy when you take away other horses. They'll whinny, charge the fences, and pace up and down, sometimes for days. This

Buddies, a herd of two. They're well-broke backyard horses. Not a day passes that they aren't fondled by a kid or two and harassed by dogs and cars. But you'll notice who they look for when they want company.

need for company is one good reason to have corrals available.

Some horses will only work for you in a herd. These are called herd-sour, or herd-bound. A related term, barn-sour, is the name for a horse that won't leave home. He understands his stall or pasture as part of his herd and refuses to leave. With either a barn-sour or a herd-bound horse, you'll need to haul to different locations to do a lot of riding that doesn't start and stop at familiar places. Almost any backyard horse will become barn-sour to some extent since so much riding is necessarily out and back. But firmness will cure most of this problem.

Hunger is a powerful motivator of horses too, though until it reaches the critical stages, it doesn't compete with the need for company. Because a horse's metabolism is geared for frequent small meals, horses like to eat all the time. Confined to good pasture and fed grain, they balloon up fast. Nowadays horses suffer many health problems because of the ease with which they get fat, though on the dry grasses of the plains where they evolved, this problem probably wasn't serious.

For the backyard owner, hunger can be a behavior problem as well as a health problem. You'll notice that your horse's attention to your commands isn't nearly as rapt as his attention to a good flake of hay. A

regular feeding schedule, usually early in the morning and late in the evening, will accustom your horse to forgetting about food most of the day, and it will help you command his attention when you want it. But this won't be a permanent change in his thinking.

If your children ride, even your well-broke horse will usually exploit the chance to grab a mouthful of grass now and then, and he'll quickly learn the habit of eating more than moving. You'll have to correct this minor discipline problem firmly and consistently. Your horse has to learn that when it's time to eat, he can eat; when it's time to work, it's time to work.

Hunger patterns can annoy you in other ways, too. If your pasture is poor, your horses won't suffer it long before they hunt food elsewhere. They'll lean over your fences until the wires or poles fall down. They'll pick the locks on your gates, and if they get loose, they'll gorge themselves on your lawn or the neighbor's corn patch. When you're riding, there comes a point when hungry horses can think of nothing but their stomachs.

You can use the hunger instinct in your favor. Most horses are suckers for grain, and grain becomes the usual device for catching cagey horses. Also, when you bring home a new horse, the fact that you visibly provide him with feed will lodge firmly in his brain and will help develop the dependency on you that leads to a good working relationship.

Many owners think it's fun to hand-feed sugar cubes or to keep a pocket full of goodies for their horses. I disagree. Hand feeding teaches a horse disrespect. He begins to see you as the candy-man, and if you disappoint him, he gets mad. Keep food, work, and lovin' separate.

Running is another part of a horse's natural makeup. You may have heard stories about horses that had to be hammered into line because they were so mean. There probably are some of those, but most horses aren't fighters; they're runners. Any kind of trouble gives them the same thought that runs through a wily whitetail deer's mind: "Let's get the heck out of here."

When horses can't run, they panic. That's when they buck or, as a last resort, fight.

It is this running instinct that makes horses dangerous. When panicked, they become incredibly strong, stupid, and pain-resistant. They'll hurt themselves, and they'll hurt you.

Trainers over the centuries have devised techniques that help horses learn without triggering this instinctive running behavior. The old-time bronc riders didn't avoid it, they just fought their way through it with no real plan and some skilled riding. They stirred up quite a romantic dust cloud around themselves too, but if you peer closely through the cloud, you'll notice that bronc riders mainly died young or gave up the sport after a few rough years.

Another aspect of herd psychology that will affect your working relationship with horses is their reproductive urges. Mares are famous for being unpredictable when in heat, which is almost a week out of every month from early spring through late fall. A well-schooled mare, however, will work for you in spite of her moods. One of mine will squeal and tease day and night when she's penned, but under saddle she's all business. Young, green mares will be the most troublesome when they should be working, but any mare can be trouble in a herd simply because she excites the geldings or your neighbor's stud colt. Some geldings will repeatedly mount and service a mare, while others will just fight each other for the chance to be the mare's best friend for a week. No matter what the action is, heats can be troublesome, and mares can be bruised as a result.

There are also occasional mares for whom the unpregnant state is unbearable. Old Kewpie Doll from up the river went through fences and corrals to get in with a stud who lives miles away. She had a lovely black colt the next spring.

Despite her idiosyncrasies, a good mare is hard to beat, and owners who won't have one are often passing up a good deal. Most people, however, prefer geldings. Within a few months of being gelded, male horses lose the raging excitement of their unaltered state and from then on are the most stable personalities. As far as endurance or trainability is concerned, there isn't as much difference between geldings and mares as between individuals of the same sex.

Stallions are just about out of the question for backyard horse owners. First, they will cause more trouble on a regular basis than any mare or gelding is capable of. Yes, some stallions are peaceable keepers, but they are few. When the urge is upon him, a stallion can become a powerful and unmanageable dynamo in a matter of seconds. An acquaintance's big stallion showed up in my dad's yard early one June morning, shrieking for mares. By the time the dust settled, we learned he had torn up fences, geldings, and himself in an eight-mile spree. Most days this stallion could be trusted to carry the grandkids around the yard, but this was June, and his libido had the best of him.

Such troubles aren't the only reason for backyard owners to forego stallions. We just don't have the facilities, the work, or the purpose for having them in the first place. Stud horses require extra-strong fences and corrals. You need plenty of work to keep that burning energy worn down or plenty of mares for him to breed. If you have neither, you are subjecting the horse to a real torment just for the sake of saying you keep a stud.

Breeding should have a purpose beyond furthering pet pollution. This part is stewardship. To be a responsible owner of a stallion, you must learn pedigrees, performance, and breeding techniques. Backyard horsemen can seldom do all of this and seldom have a reason to. Buy a gelding or mare. Let the professionals have the trouble of keeping stallions.

Individual personalities

While it isn't realistic to fit every member of the entire horse species into a few pigeon holes, I intend to do just that for the sake of giving you some idea of the range of horse personalities. Some of these behaviors are undoubtedly strictly genetic, while others arise when heredity and environment collide. There are variations within types, and there are variations in intelligence on top of personality differences, so remember that what I say here is only a foundation.

The first group I've come to call the nervous performers. These horses are nervous and quirky, usually lesser powers within a herd and, in my experience, more often mares than males. They will watch for horse-eaters all the time, and flee everything new. Tied, they are jumpy, and while you're riding, they're tense and sometimes explosive until their energy begins to focus on the task at hand.

I like nervous performers, not for their nervousness, but because they're performers. These horses, carefully handled, will work their hearts out. It almost seems as if they're afraid to do something wrong. Many of them seem to have great stamina, maybe because of their nervous energy. One that comes to mind is a nice, refined mare who is not a bit friendly or interested in people while being shod, petted, or saddled. When she's carrying a rider she's all business, and there isn't a thing she won't learn. I've seen her walk better-conditioned horses into the ground day after day.

Once you recognize the nervous performer's quirks, you'll find him learning things fast. But for the beginning rider, he may be a challenge and possibly a danger. Wrong moves from you can elicit explosive

reactions, and because they panic so easily, nervous performers can hurt you. Luckily you can single out this personality more easily than some others before you buy: watch this horse being handled by the seller, and you'll notice the same quickness of movement you'd expect if a stranger were doing the handling. If the horse looks as if he's charged with electricity, be wary. If his reactions scare you, you should look elsewhere.

On the other hand, if you are a confident rider with competitive performance in mind, give this horse another look. If he has the build to accomplish what you want, he may take you to the top. Just remember that even after you develop a good working relationship, you can never be careless around him. He won't attack you, but he may hurt you.

The second group is the chargers, and I didn't invent the name. Most horsemen know what others mean when they say a horse is "chargey." These horses are aggressive workers that can become completely unlikable if their worst characteristics win out. Chargers are the horses that insist on being at the head of a group, even if they can't walk fast enough to get there. They may become hot-headed if they don't get to the front. They may look for excuses to bite or kick nearby horses. Chargers become hot-headed when you work them in close quarters. They will develop a hard mouth in a hurry, because if you push them at all in training, they want to run madly, and you will be constantly hauling them in to start over again. Chargers will test your nerve. They pay little attention to the ground and simply bull their way through whatever shows up—trees, rocks, rivers, or brush. They will definitely test your patience as you try to figure out why you have to ask so many times for only a little cooperation.

But charginess can be an asset. Channel it and you'll have a powerful horse on your hands, perhaps a good steer-roping horse, jumper, cow horse, or endurance horse. As he gets older, much of his charginess may go underground if hard use and good schooling keep it controlled. If your skill and patience hold up, there is nothing wrong with a chargy horse.

Ironically chargers may be the quietest, nosiest, friendliest pets on your place when you aren't riding. There is no justice.

The charger who gets away with his worst impulses turns into what I call a prancer-dancer. I won't keep one of these myself, though when I was younger I thought it pretty heroic to travel sideways and up-and-down more than forward.

Prancer-dancers wear themselves out performing a variety of pawings, floppings, foamings, poundings, and sidelings. None are cute, comfortable, or particularly useful.

A type I like much better than a prancer is what I call the deadhead. These are frequently referred to as "born broke." They don't mind anything you do to them as long as you don't disturb their slumber. These are the horses that kids can break to ride, the horses that make good dude and pack horses. They usually aren't very bright, but they aren't mean or flighty either. This lesser intelligence combined with a mellow attitude works great for most backyard uses.

While the deadhead isn't likely to hurt you, he may never excite you either. I remember one I was training to pack. Five minutes into the training program, I crossed a creek and instead of dallying around my saddle horn, I just held the lead rope in one hand. He pulled away from me and realizing he was loose, trotted away. Now a nervous performer or a chargy horse in the same situation would probably have done something fast and dumb, like trying to unload the packs. Old deadhead, however, couldn't be troubled that much, so he just kept on trotting. I caught him in a hundred yards, and that was the only objection he ever made to a lifetime of carrying odd bundles.

I like deadheads for some things. I've found them highly dependable in mountain country and for cow work if things don't get too technical. They have some drawbacks, however. One is that no matter how much time you invest in them, they don't seem to improve much beyond the broke-and-usable stage. Another is that if they ever do get a whole idea in their minds, there's no talking them out of it. A deadhead who takes up kicking or bucking, for example, may become a confirmed kicker or bucker. Once I hurried a deadhead along too fast and threw on a load of old tires before he had sufficient notice. He broke down a gate, smashed a barn door, and knocked himself down three or four times. Eventually he became a dude horse and carried hunters quietly for a month or more. One day the outfitter needed an extra packhorse, so he loaded this deadhead. You guessed it: halfway to camp old Sleepy dumped the whole load in a half-mile spree. Yes, he was carrying the eggs.

The knothead category includes some knotheads that are made and some that are born. A knothead may not be dangerous; he may just be no fun to work with. He may fight you one day and ignore you the next. He may be so disrespectful of you he refuses to bend to your commands. He may be so timid you cannot make any training

progress without blind runaways. And there are knotheads that definitely are dangerous. Despite all the stories about what tender loving care can do, I firmly believe that some horses like being vicious and not necessarily within a herd. I started a gelding once that loved to buck. A little bucking goes a long way with me, but what I really feared was his habit of reaching out in mid-buck with a hind leg and kicking the nearest corral posts with deadly accuracy. If he had bucked me off—I never gave him the chance—he'd have kicked out my brains in mid-air. He also couldn't be hand fed, couldn't be approached on the right side, and wouldn't settle down under the quietest of care. Had he been abused? No. He was well cared for on a small place and accustomed to humans, traffic, and other horses. He was just plain mean.

One type of horse that seems prone to knotheadedness is the horse raised away from other horses and in a small area. Their knotheadedness may have something to do with never learning herd manners. I'm sure there are many exceptions to this pattern, but I've seen it enough times to believe it is a pattern.

If you end up with a horse you think may be a knothead, your first step should be to visit a professional trainer. Perhaps a month or two of the right use will straighten out this horse. If step one doesn't work, step two is to get rid of the horse any way you can without hurting someone else. There are plenty of good horses out there. You owe no loyalty to knotheads.

And that, finally, brings us to the subject of the good ones. These are the horses we all want, and despite all the time I've devoted to these negative types, the good ones far outnumber the bad. Good ones are alert but calm, probably nervous or troublesome when facing new things but willing to be talked or trained out of their silliness. With practice they become steady performers, and you can count on them to keep learning through their whole life. They are willing workers, and they have the mental toughness to carry them far beyond what you might expect from their physical condition. They are limited only by their athletic abilities and their rider's knowledge and skill. The good ones may be rope horses, for example, that know the difference between the roper and the roper's kids. Chip is such a horse, an excellent steer-roping horse who can still be puffing from running the steers while he quietly carries one or more kids. He will load anywhere into any vehicle, travel rock-steady in any rough country, and stand for any stranger or friend to catch. He will pack anything you can lash on his back. His

breeding? No one knows for sure, though either a quarter horse or Morgan fancier could make a case for him, and either would be proud to do just that. He is also darn well built, one of the few grade horses that should have been left a stallion.

Whether you're setting out to buy a horse or have already bought one, this horse psychology business will be a big part of your life from now on. Like other aspects of horsemanship, it will take a long time to understand, and neither you nor I nor anyone else will ever understand it all. The problem you face as a beginner is having so much to watch for and so little experience to help you interpret what you see.

If you've already bought but don't like what you have, remember that many personalities become tolerable as you work with them. I've known extreme nervous performers who, with steady and correct handling, became kids' horses by the time they reached their mid-teens. I've known deadheads that became so dependable their lesser intelligence is no longer a factor worth considering. If you spend enough time with your horse either you or he may improve to the point where tolerance occurs.

Remember too that a horse may show two different personalities, one you see from the ground, the other from the saddle. One may

What's between those ears will decide a lot of things for you. Deadhead, knothead . . . or maybe a sweet-tempered genius?

be tolerable, even pleasant, and the other unbearable. Remember that there is a difference between the horse's personality and the rider's mistakes. Finally remember that no horse is perfect.

I want to end this chapter with a story of two big geldings, Clyde and Gus, both sorrels, both good, strong, grade quarter horses, both broke to ride at age three. Looking at them side by side, you'd have thought them twins.

Clyde never bucked a moment of his life. He was a fast walker, a chargy runner, almost dangerous in a tight situation because he had no patience at all. The first time I packed him was in the middle of a trip when another horse got sore ribs, so the whole packing game came as a surprise to him. I expected a mid-mountain rodeo, but Clyde never made a wrong move.

Clyde was impossible to shoe, a two-man job every time, and none of my friends would come back to help with the job a second time. Clyde went into a foaming panic at any kind of rope around his feet, and he never quit fighting those

ropes—which were necessary to shoe him—until he was burned and exhausted.

Gus bucked like he meant it a few times while being broke, and the only time he was ever packed successfully, he unloaded the hay bales just as they arrived in camp. I tried packing boxes on him, but he stomped them to slivers before I could even get them on him.

Gus is a delight to shoe. He picks up his feet on command and holds them up as long as the shoer wants. He doesn't mind ropes under his feet or tail. He is a fast walker, a chargy runner, and apt to get angry in tight spots, though as he ages, this anger is gradually disappearing. Kids can now ride him safely if they don't run him, and he has been used as a dude horse more than once.

Both of these horses could be caught anywhere with a handful of grain. Both would hang around any humans if there were any chance of a handout. Both were powerful and aggressive against other horses.

To get the best out of them, you had to get to know them, and that took years.

chapter seven
Health and Feeding: The Basics

We've all heard of people starving their animals, and we've perhaps wondered how these atrocities can occur in an educated land of plenty. But while starving them is among the worst things people do to animals, there are other forms of abuse and neglect too. Some result from deliberate cruelty, but more often, they simply reflect ignorance. There may be times when animals must suffer because our energies are needed to save human lives—during natural disasters like hurricanes, floods, or severe blizzards, for instance. But there is no excuse for abuse or neglect from ignorance.

Equine health is an extremely complex subject but it is often made more complex than necessary by people who have a vested interest in doing so. If you can read well enough to pass a driver's test and think well enough to get up for breakfast, you can take care of a horse's health needs.

General condition

In feeding and caring for your horse you are trying to maintain him at a point of physical condition that allows him to feel good and tolerate his normal workload without undue stress. This may sound simple so far, but it's subject to many variables.

With most horse owners, underfeeding to the point of starvation isn't a problem. We usually have sense enough to lay out more feed when bones begin to show. But for some reason we've come to believe that overfeeding is a form of affection. When we think that way, we're wrong.

A travel brochure, produced by some state office, shows three horses perched on a mountainside in summer-green Montana. Those horses are so fat the saddles splay out flat on the horses' backs. If those horses had to travel any distance to pose in that picture,

Normally, a horse showing this much hip and rib is too thin. This horse, however, is a well-fed endurance horse. He's thin because he's in top shape.

I pity them, because their lungs and hearts must have been in agony. I knew a good little horse in just such an obese condition that suffered a heart attack and fell over on his rider a few miles from home. And riders of those overfed horses can't be much better off, though different parts of their anatomies suffer as their legs straddle those huge stomachs.

The idea that fat is desirable doesn't come only from a misguided sense of kindness. It is promoted in many cases by horse-show judges and by commercial feed producers. These shiny horses we see in full-color ads are round as can be; that's permissible if at the same time those horses are getting plenty of strenuous exercise. But in your backyard operation, fat and exercise don't usually go together.

We should want for our horses what we want for ourselves. We don't expect our bodies to withstand a twenty-mile hike or a three-mile run if we are 30 percent overweight. Most of us fear such situations, knowing just how bad the consequences can be. In fact, we worry so much about keeping our weight down that pills, books, and machines, all purporting to guarantee us a streamlined-for-health-and-sex physique, are popular consumer goods everywhere.

While we can't put our horses on the jogging trampoline, we can control their weight. If your whole horse viewed from either the side or the rear seems to be built only in round chunks, he is probably too fat, though in horses as in people, builds do reflect inherited characteristics. Horses

The opposite extreme—a mare whose broad back, cresty neck, and fleshy shoulders demonstrate what good feed and no work can come to. She's healthy and probably doesn't mind her condition at all, but a sudden dose of hard work will be rough on her system and maybe fatal.

with some pony background, for example, will usually be round even in good shape. If your horse is built only of angles, he is already too thin. Somewhere in between is what you want, with muscle delineation visible but flesh still there in quantity.

A healthy horse won't look either fat or skinny. His hips will be rounded, though you'll be able to feel the big pelvic bone on each side. There will be a dimple at the top of his hips, like a little channel running down to the tail. His ribs may show when the light hits them just right, but they'll have flesh on them. His withers will be fairly angular rather than rounded, his neck neither crested with fat nor wasting away at the base (ewe-necked).

Look at a good endurance horse some time and you'll see one extreme. He will be all angles, but his hard muscle tone makes him look that way. A horse that thin and not in training is weak. Look at a good halter horse also used for performance events, and you'll see the opposite story. Judges like fat, so this horse will be round, but he may also be in excellent physical condition for participation in strenuous events. Again, if a horse is this fat and not in training, he is weak.

While fat-or-thin judgments are the most common way of evaluating general condition, you can learn from the condition of a horse's coat, too. In summer, the darker bays, sorrels, chestnuts, and palominos will develop a natural shine on short, fine hairs lying flat and close. Dirt may obscure the shine and months of hot sun dry and fade it, but brushing will bring it up. Lighter-colored horses won't shine as much. Some, like dappled appys or roans, will have a coarser coat, but these too should be of short hairs lying flat and close in summer.

A horse in poor condition in summer will have a coarse coat and an apathetic attitude. He may have trouble shedding out winter hair, particularly under his belly. This could merely reflect poor feeding or untreated worms. Both are easy to fix. He could also be suffering from unknown illnesses, skin parasites, or vitamin deficiencies. Such things may not be as readily diagnosed and treated. If he has a poor coat, find out why.

In winter, horse coats vary from the 3-inch mat from eyes to hooves of the hardy Shetland, to the fuzzed-up ½-inch coat of a grain-fed hotblood. Some horses seem impervious to the cold if we judge by their short winter coats, but I think that their bodies don't really make that decision. Heredity dictates a short coat, and the animal suffers. It is especially important to have a roof, a windbreak, and often extra feed for fine-coated individuals.

The healthy winter coat will be thick, even, and resilient. On a cold morning the hairs will be standing straight out with the extra-long guard-hairs touched with frost. If you are buying a horse in the winter, or just checking your own horse's condition, look to see if the coat looks alive and if the coat is in about the same condition as that of other horses getting the same feed and shelter.

Working condition is part of a horse's general health, but it's more too. Working condition is a measure of stamina, and it isn't likely that you'll get a clear picture of this in most buying situations. It would be nice to ride the animal at speed or in some hills so you can judge his stamina, but in most cases as a buyer you'll have to assume working condition can be developed if the horse's general condition is good. Once you own the animal, you'll become aware of his ability to build stamina, and during the riding season, you'll try to improve his stamina as much as possible.

Don't expect a horse to gallop for miles without showing the effects. Any horse will begin sweating almost immediately under heavy work, and his breathing rate will increase. His recovery rate tells the tale of conditioning. If you really want to get serious, take a horse's heartbeat with a stethoscope, count his breathing rate, and then exercise him vigorously for fifteen or twenty minutes. Once you stop, he should regain his normal readings in approx-

imately ten minutes. Use common sense, however. Don't expect him to recover in ten minutes from a five-mile run the first time out in the spring.

Be wary of extremely labored breathing, breathing that has a raspy or roaring sound, or a horse that seems to fade away after a mile or two of walking or jogging. Any horse that is well fed should be able to shuffle right along over eight or ten miles of easy terrain even on the first spring ride. If he can't, he could be sick, older than you think, or crippled in some way that doesn't show. If he has raspy or roaring breathing, he is either sick enough to be at the vet's immediately or unusable as a result of past illness or injury.

How much time does it take to keep a horse in good working condition? This depends on a variety of factors. Generally speaking, horses build stamina faster and keep it longer than humans do. This doesn't mean horses can be expected to perform once-a-year miracles, however. And some horses can take much harder work with less preparation than others. Such toughness varies more between individuals than between breeds or sizes. Let me give an example.

While writing this chapter, I helped on a twenty-five mile cattle drive through some brushy, semi-mountainous terrain. The horses included an average-size appy mare, age seventeen; a big appy gelding, age five; a big crossbred gelding, age nine; a medium-size quarter horse gelding, age five; a 13-hand pony, age seven; and a medium-size crossbred mare, age twenty-seven. The two mares had had the least preparation. The big appy and the big crossbred had been on several four-hour expeditions, a branding, another cattle drive, and a bunch of short rides all during the previous six weeks.

The results of this twelve-hour ordeal? The pony was the most energetic at the end of the day, but all of the horses, including the ancient mare, were still working honestly when we quit. The quarter horse gelding carried the most weight but still had go-power like the rest, and he was the one that might surprise breed fanatics, since he was the round, heavily-muscled type built for power and quick speed, not endurance. He was also an exceptionally fast walker.

If you were to keep your horse in condition to make this trip without undue stress, you would probably need ten or more hours per week of reasonably strenuous work—some hill climbing, some running, some quick stops and starts. This isn't possible for most of us, however. A couple of these horses hadn't had ten strenuous

hours of work in the previous month. A good figure for us backyard types to shoot for might be six or eight hours of lighter work spread over three or four days. In early spring these would be hours of walking and jogging for the first couple of weeks. After that they should include hills, running, or pulling something to build wind and muscle tone. This same regimen will have to continue through the riding season. And if you do continue it, your horse will gradually become pretty hard—not endurance competition hard, but hard enough that the long days you give him on occasion won't hurt him at all. In fact after the first few weeks, you'll want to put in those long days just for variety and further conditioning.

A final conditioning consideration is caring for the endless string of little dings a horse gets from bugs, fences, other horses, and sometimes, it seems, just from the air they breathe. If he is scabby with bug bites, if his legs are knotted with sores, if his ribs are raw from cinch rings, you are not fulfilling part of your ownership responsibility. Take care of these things, too, to keep your animal's condition and attitude sound.

Feeding

Basic health depends more on what you feed and how much you feed than on any one other thing. While horse nutrition at the biochemical level is extremely complex, and while knowing such things may be a worthwhile goal in your long-range plans to improve your horsemanship, you can keep a healthy horse with a minimum knowledge of feeding.

If your pasture is in good condition, your horses will usually stay healthy enough that you won't have to be ashamed of them, assuming you lock them up enough hours per day to prevent obesity. But if that pasture is never fertilized and never given a chance to regenerate itself, a feeding horse gradually removes the best, most nutritious grasses. If needed nutrients aren't in the grass, they won't get into your horse, and his condition will show it. Also, soils can lack essential minerals. (Your county agent can test soil for you.) Combine this possibility with over-grazing and you have potential for serious health problems.

Hay is a real problem for backyard owners. We feed it all winter long and in many cases most of the summer, too. But like pasture grasses, hay reflects the nutritional characteristics of the soil it comes from. It also varies greatly in protein content and preservation qualities. You must do your hay buying and feeding with eyes and nose wide open.

Buy the best hay raised in your area. More specifically, buy the best alfalfa hay if it is available. Old-timers didn't feed alfalfa giving various reasons, but they were wrong. Compared to the lightweight grasses, alfalfa is a much better feed. As my vet once said: "The only alfalfa that hurt him is the alfalfa he didn't get."

In northern states alfalfa is cut two or three times per year. The first cutting often has the highest protein content, but the second and third are desirable for horses because there is less chance of rain on the hay, and because there will be fewer weeds in the hay itself. Horses pass weed seeds through their systems intact, ready to spring up in unwanted places.

Not only does it make sense to buy alfalfa from a nutritional standpoint, but you will find that in many cases it is no more expensive per bale, and you can often feed up to 20 percent less weight per animal. That translates to money saved and less chance of the hay-belly horses get from stuffing themselves on low-quality hay.

There are two drawbacks to alfalfa. First, it can have heavy stems if left too long before cutting, and horses don't like these. If they can survive just nibbling the leaves

75

and leaving the stems, they will, and you'll have bought tons of waste. This problem is usually solved by buying second or third cutting. The second drawback is that alfalfa is prone to be dusty, and it will mold if harvested damp or stored improperly. Both dust and mold will cause your horse serious respiratory problems.

You can avoid poor hay by checking for good green color on the inside of the bale. Hay left out in the sun loses color quickly. Dig into the guts of a bale for the true test of its quality. If possible, shake out a few flakes to see how much dust was baled, and finally, use your nose to check for mold. These checks apply to any type of hay.

If alfalfa isn't available, other species will serve you well. Orchard grass is a common irrigated hay with good protein content and fine stems that horses will really clean up. They also like the old standbys, timothy and June grass. But don't try to feed enough of these grass hays to keep a horse fat. Keep the quantity down and supplement with grain or you'll have a horse with a huge belly but poor flesh. One reason old-timers got by on grass hay was that they were more than likely working their horses all winter and feeding significant quantities of grain along with the hay. In that situation, the hay provided roughage more than nutrition.

Successful hay storage depends upon two things. The hay must be dry when you buy it, and it must be kept out of the weather but with plenty of air circulation. Throwing a sheet of plastic over the stack is a common practice, but hay will mold this way as its own moisture condenses on the underside of the sheet. Also, plastic doesn't last long (even hay stems will puncture it), and it will soon leak rainwater and melting snow. Some of this leakage flows down through the stack and starts rot. Some of it condenses under the plastic and increases mold and rot on the top surface of the stack.

When you consider that you are paying a minimum of $65 per ton (1980s' prices) and perhaps two or three times that in some places, the way to keep hay expense down is to keep it under a roof either in a barn or in a pole shed. In either, you can stack the hay with airspace between bales without worrying about the stack falling down, since the poles or walls will hold things together. The next best method is to build a tight stack outside, throw some old tires on top, put a couple of poles or planks on the tires, and cinch down a good quality tarp big enough to extend five or six feet down the sides of the stack. The tires will keep your tarp up off the hay, and the poles will keep the tarp from drooping on the stack ends. Punch grommets every 24 inches around the tarp, and use all of them to tie

Two different kinds of feed-bunks: The upper one will feed two horses who don't like each other, or up to four who do. It is 5' x 8' x 32". With air space beneath it and made of treated lumber, it will last many years. The lower bunk will feed one horse. It is 3' x 5' x 32". The back is higher so that if the bunk is set away from the fence, there is still only one way into it for the horse. Nobody else can steal off his plate.

down. If you cannot set grommets (grommet kits are inexpensive and simple to use), roll a 2-inch stone into the tarp's edge and tie it there with twine. This will provide a secure holding-spot for your tie-down twines or ropes. Do this also at 2-foot intervals.

Although this method will serve you well, your enemy will be the wind. It will whip the tarp to shreds if it can get the least corner to start on, and it will balloon the tarp during the worst rainstorm of the season and allow rain to blow underneath. You can get by with a good tarping job, but you're better off with the right kind of building.

Plan on feeding your horse 20 pounds per day for a 1000-pound animal. This should be divided among two or three feedings per day, 7 to 10 pounds per feeding. After a month or so you'll know if your horse is gaining, losing, or maintaining weight. Twenty pounds is only a starting place; some 1200-pound horses eat no more than some 800-pound horses. Usually long, lean horses are less efficient food converters than the short, round horses, but only experience will show if this is true for your individual animals. The amount of feed a horse needs is another economic consideration when you buy. Why buy a horse that is expensive to keep if a more efficient horse will do the job you have in mind?

When it comes time to feed horses, many people just throw hay on the ground. If you have space enough to continually move the feeding spot, if the ground is well-drained so it is never muddy, if there's no accumulation of manure where you feed, this method is adequate. Building a hay bunk for each animal is better since there will be far less waste and mess, and your horses will not reinfect themselves with parasites as fast.

Despite the advice of commercial feed manufacturers and animal nutrition experts who assert the need for several pounds of grain per day plus supplements, I have never felt bad about wintering horses on alfalfa hay alone. As long as they get both quality and quantity, horses maintain their coat condition, fat level, and alert attitude. They shed out on schedule in the spring, and they pick up working condition rapidly with use. I have, however, seen horses wintering on hay alone grow thin, shaggy, and apathetic. Quality is critical, and when it is questionable at all, you have to take the next step and supplement hay with grain. This holds true not only for wintering horses, but also for horses working steadily, for pregnant mares, and for young, growing horses. One caution: too much hot feed in the form of grain mixes, supplements, and specialty feeds can make young horses grow so fast that serious muscle and bone problems result.

Oats are the old favorite horse feed. Horses love them, and anything from a quart and up per day will affect condition. If your horse is getting daily workouts of an hour or more, start by giving him a quart of oats on working days. After a few weeks adjust the amount according to his condition. Crimped or rolled oats are a little more digestible, but there is relatively less by volume so you'll want to measure by weight rather than container size. The reason you don't feed grain on non-working days is that horses get an illness called azoturia, or Monday-morning sickness,

when they don't work off a day's grain ration. Of course this isn't likely with smaller quantities of grain.

Barley is a hotter, or more energetic, feed. It is also excellent for horses, but since it is hotter you'll want to watch its quantity carefully. Buy it rolled or crimped. Corn and wheat aren't usually fed alone to horses, but a rolled corn-oats-barley-molasses mix, known as COB or three-way, is fairly common. It is excellent feed in terms of taste, digestibility, and quality, but too much of it will have your horse dancing on the ragged edge of a frenzy all the time.

You aren't being kind when you pump your horse full of hot feed and don't allow him the chance to work it off. I once shod the after-effects on a race horse who had pawed away the outer shell of her hoof. A combination of a racing diet, weeks of confinement, and no work had made her insane. Even regrown, the hoof was a mess, and the horse was crippled for life.

When you are conditioning a horse for extreme stress—endurance riding, for example—you'll be feeding 10 or more pounds of hot feeds per day, plus specially prepared feed supplements, so potent they are fed in increments of tablespoons. Distrust the man who says your backyard horse needs this kind of diet on a regular basis. That man probably has an investment in a feed company.

Grain storage on a small scale isn't difficult. Like hay, grain needs to be kept dry. Good quality garbage cans will do the trick and discourage mice too. An old chest-style deep-freeze is a good container too, if you can keep it away from the horses and if you horse-proof it with a strong latch. Never be careless about storing grain. Horses will literally eat themselves to death if they can get at your grain supply, and they can be pretty clever about opening cans and latches.

Since horses like grain so much, they become aggressive when you bring it out. They may push you, nip you, and fight each other with you underfoot. Don't let them develop these nasty habits. Dump grain in separate feed boxes in an empty pen or corral. Let the horses in when you're ready.

Worms

Internal parasites, worms in everyday language, are a fact of horse life. Luckily there are plenty of effective ways to control them, so the only thing preventing you from keeping the worm population down is you. Some of the de-wormers like injections and tube-wormers should be administered by a vet unless you are trained and confident

with the techniques; others you can administer by yourself. Powdered wormers generally work only for horses so grain-greedy nothing will stop them from wolfing down the groceries. The simplest and surest wormers are the paste types that come in large plastic syringes. You just put the syringe tip into the corner of the horse's mouth and push the plunger.

Talk to a vet about the most efficient method and brands, switch types occasionally to avoid developing a local strain of resistant worms. Be religious about worming each animal: twice a year is the minimum, four to six times is desirable. Some people worm every thirty days, but it seems that if this were completely effective, there would soon be no reason to worm at all. At any rate, worming is a must and, considering the benefits of improved health and reduced hay consumption, easily pays for itself. Recent research links worms to weakened intestinal functioning, a probable cause of colic. The cost of one vet's call for colic will buy a lot of worm medicine.

Wormers may work on the earthworm population in your garden if you use the manure for fertilizer. If you are an organic purist, lock up your horse for a couple of days after worming, and haul that manure to the city dump. Of course, if you don't

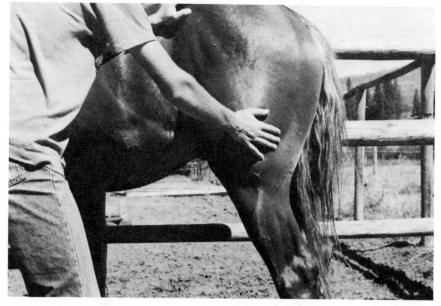

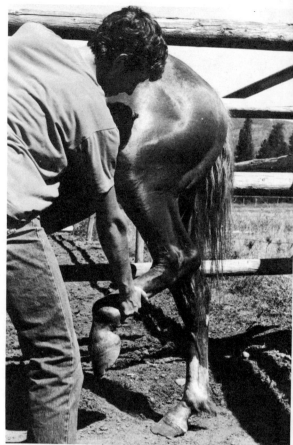

Picking up a hind foot safely is done by keeping your near hand on the hip, and running the other hand down the leg. Keep your body close to the horse.

Keeping that near hand at the hip, grasp the lower leg and pull forward. A horse can kick you at this point, but not with any force. He has to come forward to reach you, and you'll have time to move. If he kicks straight back, you are clear anyway.

want any artificial chemicals at all, you won't want to use these medicines. But your horse deserves good parasite control, and I've never seen any evidence that the old methods of feeding plug tobacco or poplar bark really worked.

Hooves and teeth

I'll offer some common day-to-day tips on hoof care here, but I suggest you read much more widely on this subject. There are many excellent books on the subject (see Appendix). One I like very much for its completeness and succinct style is *The Complete Horseshoeing Guide* by Robert F. Wiseman, (University of Oklahoma Press, 1968).

If you keep your place clean, your horse is not likely to pick up foreign objects in his feet. Check frequently anyway. Get in the habit of checking each time you saddle up. Give a quick dig with a hoof pick and you'll clear out enough mud and manure to get a

good look. Any large objects such as stones or sticks will pop right out too. A side benefit of this frequent inspecting is that your horse grows accustomed to having his feet handled, something your shoer will appreciate.

Foot injuries, particularly those on the bottom surface, are nothing to try saving money on. The foot stands all day in things that make infectious little bugs just wriggle with delight, and horses don't tolerate infection well. You might save a few bucks by waiting a day or two; you might also lose the horse. Get a vet.

Whether or not your horse needs shoes depends on the terrain, on how much use he's getting, and on his natural hoof quality. If the hoof material is thick and solid and if the horse doesn't mind the gravel test mentioned earlier, you can probably ride in soft ground or good arena surfaces for a long time with no trouble. If you can leave him barefooted, you should. But if you ride on hard-surfaced roads, if the country you cover is rocky, if the hooves wear down

Step ahead, past the horse's tail. Get a firm grip on the lower leg. With your near arm lock his hock against your ribs. Don't pull the leg out to the side as you will off-balance the horse. The horse will be more comfortable if you hold the foot as low as possible. An average man can out-muscle the average horse in this position, since the horse's muscles are made for pushing back, not pulling forward. Step sideways and set the foot down to release. Don't just drop it if you can help it.

rapidly or can't pass the gravel test, or if you are conditioning for serious work, shoe your horse. A horse with sore feet, like an over-extended hiker, will survive, but he won't think about much else. You won't get the best out of him, you may do him long-term damage, and you are definitely abusing him. Good shoeing is another one of those things that separates the horseman from the casual owner. Shoeing shows that you're willing to do what needs to be done.

Sometimes shoeing seems surrounded with the mystery and price tag of the medical professional, and there is no doubt that it can be complicated and difficult work. But it isn't magic. If you wish to save money in the long run, learn to shoe. There are shoers who will show you how, and you can learn by watching others. Wiseman's book is great for beginners. Use common sense, and don't make your first blind stab at it on Friday night expecting to be on a mountain trail the next day. Study and practice deliberately over time. Learn trimming first. Then practice shaping some shoes. Obtain the right tools. Good ones will pay for themselves in no time and will make the job easier. If you can't afford an anvil at first, a chunk of full-size railroad track makes a workable substitute. Practice on a horse that will put up with the handling, and be darned sure you know what you're

doing when you drive that first nail.

It is possible to permanently injure a horse by poor shoeing, but the danger isn't as great as you might think. Don't learn to shoe on your barrel, jumping, or rope horse, since animals doing fast, strenuous work need skillful shoeing. Start with the old pack horse or the kids' horse. Don't leave your novice shoeing efforts on the horse more than six weeks, and pull any shoeing job after eight weeks.

While the old saw "no foot, no horse" sums up the down-to-earth end of horse care, taking care of the teeth can be as important. Teeth don't need several treatments per year, but they do need occasional checking. If they're in bad shape, they can make your horse lose weight, get sick, or at least throw his head around and act silly.

Wolf teeth are a problem in some horses. They are a small tooth in the upper jaw that can get in the way of the bit and cause enough discomfort to make your horse angry whenever you use him. Your vet will pop these out easily and the horse won't miss them. If your horse seems a little head-crazy, this is one place to start checking.

A more usual tooth problem as the horse ages is the jagged edges that develop as the teeth wear down. These may keep food from

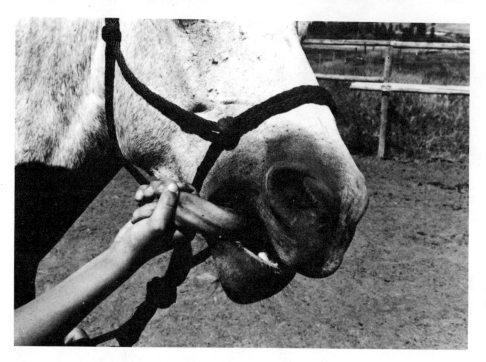

To check your horse's teeth hold the tongue, but don't try to pull it out by the roots. Stand to the side while you're doing this.

being chewed properly and thus inhibit proper digestion. They may cause sores to develop inside the cheeks too. A horse that slobbers excessively and lets a lot of food fall out of his mouth may have bad teeth. The inside surfaces of his cheeks could be so sore he can't help being a sloppy eater.

You can check for such problems by running your finger along the outside edges of the chewing teeth. Hold the horse's mouth open by pulling his tongue out to one side. He won't bite it; as long as you have hold of it, your fingers are safe inside. Honest.

A vet will "float" bad teeth for you. If the horse cooperates, floating isn't complicated. The vet uses a small rasp with a long handle and simply flattens the tooth surfaces so they fit nicely together. It doesn't hurt the horse, but you can almost feel the grinding noise on your own teeth.

Vaccinations

Many horse illnesses are transmitted from horse to horse by shared feed bunks or watering troughs. The backyard owner who never takes his horse anywhere and never has any strange horses come to his place isn't likely to have much trouble with influenza, distemper, and other infectious diseases. But vaccinations for the common diseases are inexpensive and effective and should be administered on a yearly basis anyway. For horses that travel to shows, rodeos, or any other gathering of horses, vaccinations are a must.

Along with influenza and distemper, you should vaccinate against encephalitis. Other common vaccinations are rhino-pneumonitis and tetanus. To get the job done right for your area check with your vet, and put your horse on a regular schedule. You can do the job yourself once you know the proper vaccines and dosages. Giving the shot is the easy part.

Common minor illnesses and injuries

You'd think something that has been playing the evolutionary roulette wheel for as long as horses have would be rid of all weaknesses by now, but it isn't that way at all. You need to read extensively about horse health and learn to recognize by attitude and symptoms the many things that can go wrong. More important, you need to be able to recognize that something is wrong. Here's a basic list you should become familiar with immediately.

Colic is a gastro-intestinal disorder which can come from sudden changes of diet, from worms, or from overeating. A horse with colic has a severe stomachache. He will be uninterested in food. He may bite or kick at his flanks. He may be alternately listless and restless, first standing apart from other horses, then pacing or lying down and rolling repeatedly. While some colics subside on their own, they can easily be fatal.

Call a vet or get your horse to one the moment you suspect colic. In the meantime keep the horse moving, and try not to let up. You're not being cruel; you're saving his life. Most colic is successfully treated with a combination of mineral oil administered through a stomach tube and modern pain-killing and muscle-relaxing drugs. But if your horse twists an intestine while writhing on the ground, he will die without expensive and complex surgery, and even that is not always successful.

Founder, or laminitis, is another eating-related illness. Oddly enough its symptoms appear in the horse's feet. A horse suffering an attack of founder will appear lame in all four feet though somewhat more so in the front. The hooves will feel unusually warm. If he is standing, he may attempt to rest two feet at a time, alternately trying to stand on one diagonal—front left, rear right, for example—then the other. Often he will simply lie down and be very reluctant to get up.

Founder is extremely painful for your horse and can cripple him for life. Founder is the common result of a horse's overeating grain, and it is the reason horsemen keep grain secure. Founder can also arise from over-use of soft horses. One form that is both an illness and a form of abuse by owners is grass founder, common in both ponies and short, round horses. Grass founder results simply from overeating on lush pasture. It is painful, it reoccurs more easily after the first time, and it too can eventually cripple a horse. If your horse gets into the grain bin, don't wait for the symptoms of founder to appear; call the vet immediately. Early treatment is your best hope of preventing permanent damage to your horse's feet.

Horses are also subject to colds and flus. These are characterized by listlessness, poor appetite, coughing, and runny nose. They are simple to cure with penicillin-type products and not usually serious, but they should never be allowed to linger.

As you ride your horse, there are several little things that commonly go wrong. One is a sore back. Check your horse's back after each ride by running your fingers and thumb firmly along the spine from withers to rump. If he is really sore, he will flinch and may even act as if his knees will buckle. You may need a better saddle pad; you may need to adjust the position of your saddle (a common error is to place the saddle too far forward, causing the saddle bars to ride only on their front and back tips, one end riding on the moving shoulder blade, the other burrowing into the kidneys); or you may need to be a better rider. People flopping around in the saddle or just bumping down hard at a trot often sore a back and sometimes cause big open abrasions. Too much weight over the kidneys can also cause problems. Heavily loaded saddle bags of any kind are a frequent culprit. It should be a point of pride with you never to sore your horse.

Sores also occur at the corners of the mouth. These come from heavy-handedness or from a bit and curb strap combination that pinches. A horseman will figure out what is wrong and cure it.

The same goes for cinch sores. These come from ill-fitting equipment, poor riding, or fat. That last is the first thing to guess at. You may have to make or buy woolskin pads to put around the cinch rings. You could also change the length of the cinch; try a ¾-rigged saddle intead of a full rig, or just move the saddle back a little.

But don't ignore cinch sores. They can cripple your horse and your reputation.

Possible leg and foot injuries are many and often hard to diagnose. You need to learn the "feel" of a sound leg so you'll be able to feel leg injuries when they happen. For a good rundown of common and occasional leg injuries and some comment on the care of them, read Wiseman's book as a primer.

Of all the common horse injuries the most frequent, at least in the backyard operation, involve barbed wire and rope. Barbed-wire injuries can be avoided by getting rid of barbed wire. The rope injuries aren't so easy to avoid, because they often seem to arise from owner ignorance, and ignorance is persistent. Picketing is a good practice often handled badly. It should be taught carefully over several days or weeks; it should be taught under controlled circumstances; and it should be done by one front foot rather than by the head. Among people who are short of pasture, it's a common practice to snap any old rope on the halter, tie to the closest fence or tree, and walk off. What I've just described is stupid, cruel, neglectful, and bound to get your horse at the least some nasty rope burns, which may scar him for life. Broken bones, crippling, or death can occur as the horse struggles against a rope that seems to entangle him more with every move. It goes back to what I've said elsewhere. Tie short and high. If you must picket, picket properly . . . after training and away from fences, trees, or anything that could injure the horse.

Use and abuse

Some people think every time a horse breaks into a sweat he's being abused, while others think that any time he survives the day he is being pampered. Somewhere between these extremes it's necessary to think about how your handling of a horse is affecting him, about whether you're asking for too much or asking for so little he has no reason to perform at all. I'll offer some situations, label them, and explain why I think each is abuse or use. You may not agree with all of them, but they should stimulate your thinking.

If you keep a horse in relatively clean, dry pens with enough room to romp a little, you are certainly not abusing him, even though he isn't getting the wide open spaces he may think he deserves. But if you keep him year around in a tiny space where he has only room to walk a few steps each way, where shelter is negligible, where he is constantly standing in his own filth, you are abusing him. His minimum needs are not being met, and you don't deserve him.

If your horse nips you, your reaction may be to swat him on the nose with your hand or a riding bat; that's discipline. When you start bashing him with a fist, when you hit him repeatedly with the bat, when you pick up a stick or rock and beat on him with that, you are abusing him. This would be true even if the horse hurt you severely. All you prove by brutality is that you cannot control the situation or yourself. Such abuse results more often from ignorance than from outright cruelty. A person, for one reason or another, doesn't learn to control the horse and shows his frustration by becoming brutal. Don't let anyone convince you that brutality teaches respect. Work and discipline teach respect. Pain teaches fear, and fear makes your horse even harder to work with.

Let's say you are learning to rope. The first few times in the box, your horse is too excited to be trainable. He rears, throws himself around, ignores you and the task. You absolutely cannot let him get by with this. It is dangerous, and it certainly won't let you rope. You must discipline, usually with a quick rap between the ears for the rearing offense.

Too often though a rider in that situation resorts to lashing of both ends of his horse with the lariat. People are watching, and he can't spend time just teaching the horse to stand in the box. He's committed himself to rope steers even though the horse isn't ready. Now that isn't only abusive, it's downright dumb. Why begin a training series by asking too much? Why beat the horse with the rope he isn't supposed to fear?

If you have been riding five or ten hours per week and then spend a day or two of long, hard trail hours, asking for more in a day than you'd done previously in a week, you are using your horse hard, but he can take it. Take that same horse out for the same long days after a winter of no work and poor hay, and you're abusing him. He may survive, but you have no excuse for not building him up to it.

If you spend the night at a bar and forget to feed until noon the next day, your horse will survive, but you are neglecting him. He shouldn't have to suffer for your momentary lapses of attention. But if despite reasonable care and planning you get in a tight spot on a camping trip and there isn't any horse feed, you can tie up and quit for the night anyway. That constitutes use, as does any instance where comfort and safety of the animals must be sacrificed for the safety of

humans. If you rode into that tight spot with no plan for feed, no previous knowledge of the terrain, in other words, no thought for the horse in the first place, that's abuse. The horse may not know the difference between the accidental and the avoidable, but you will. If you have a conscience, it should tweak you for the latter.

If you feed a lot of grain to build condition for hard use or to sustain a milking mare, you are treating the horse as you should. But if you simply like to feed grain and the horse develops health problems as a result, you are abusing him just as surely as if you let him go hungry. If you are careless about the quality of your winter feeding arrangements and your horse becomes thin, you are abusing him. Even if you winter your horse out on distant pastures, you are obligated to check him frequently and supplement the pasture at the first hint of trouble.

If you have picketed in a well-thought-out place, if your horse has shade and water, if he is accustomed to being picketed, and if you are available to get him out of trouble, picketing is part of reasonable care. But if you picket a questionably-trained horse in a poorly-planned place, and if you walk away for the day or night, that is abuse. You ought to have the animal taken from you by the law.

chapter eight
Going To School

Like anything else we try, training horses isn't as easy as the professionals make it seem, and we are likely to botch it at first. The chances against unaided first-time success are somewhere on the order of making a good showing at the Indy 500 the first time you ever slide down into one of those funny cars.

Whether out of vanity or ignorance or nagging economic problems, backyard horsemen seem particularly bad about overlooking this gap between themselves and the professionals, and although not all our efforts turn out to be fruitless, we do produce a high proportion of dead-end horses: horses that can be ridden, but with so many bad habits serious further training is nearly impossible.

I can't teach you all there is to know about schooling horses. I don't know it all and never will. I can give you some general schooling techniques that will make a big difference in the usability of your horse.

Send your horse to a professional trainer

The rational is really the same as sending your car to a good mechanic. Yes, it's going to cost you money, but if you aren't a practicing mechanic, the money you spend on tools and misused parts and the time you spend doing the job several times over, may be money and time you could put to better use. It's the same with horses. You could conceivably go through a half-dozen before you schooled one well enough for him to be enjoyable. Why not get the job done properly so that when the horse arrives at your home, he's ready to work for you?

True, there are "trainers" who don't do a very good job, and there are trainers who will only do careful work on the most able horses. It is possible that out of ignorance or impatience, a trainer might mess up your horse as badly as you would. You can avoid these problems, however, by getting a list of the trainer's clients and doing some telephoning. This isn't nearly as troublesome as the problems you could have with a spoiled horse.

Sometimes trainers too get into trouble in ways they can't avoid, so try not to be completely suspicious. I broke a mare once who was an angry, coiled-spring, nervous performer. This mare would not relax even in a pen alone. We called her The Coyote from her habit of pacing the fences day and night. But she had the mental quickness to make progress rapidly, and she never bucked or ran away in a panic although I felt those were things she really wanted to do. She never really walked either, but sort of hovered in a light-footed prance that kept me wondering which way she would explode.

The owner was a retired lady who had done quite a bit of riding but who certainly was no bronc rider. I warned her that this mare was volatile. The lady rode her horse a few times, was intimidated by it, and turned it over to another man who would "have it gentled in a week or two," he claimed. With spurs and speed he managed to get bucked off enough times that he soon gave the mare back with the understanding that I was the one who hadn't handled it right in the first place. The mare was sold as useless.

It is possible I didn't handle the mare right, but I had no major blow-ups with her, and though I dreaded each ride, the mare was usable for heading cross-country when I sent her home. It was my word against that of the other trainer, so the owner was at a loss to know who messed up. In any case, I doubt I'll ever see that owner again.

When you do send your horse out, insist on riding at the trainer's establishment under his or her advice for several long lessons before you bring the horse home. No matter how well you ride, you will ride differently from the trainer; it helps you and the horse if you both understand the same cues.

Listen to what the trainer says. A client of mine arrived for her first ride on a colt I'd been working and, disregarding my advice to start with a few quiet walks around the arena, kicked the colt into a run. The client wasn't as experienced as she had let on, and the melee that followed was a potential disaster, though I couldn't help laughing as the frantic client's hands flew between falling sunglasses, falling halter-top, loose reins, and saddle horn, while the stirrups flopped away from her flailing tennis shoes. It really wasn't funny though; the only reason this girl didn't get hurt was that her colt, even frightened, had a lot of common sense and was trying to stay under the rider. He wasn't getting much help. Not all problems are the trainer's fault.

I've mentioned some of the negative possibilities in trainer-client-horse relationships, but there are more-than-compensating, positive things too. A good trainer can make more progress with your horse in a month than you may in a year, because he knows the sequence of lessons to use, and he knows both the theory and the practical aspects behind the sequence. He has a reputation to uphold, and he won't jeopardize that if he can help it. He also will put in the daily hours that you may not be able to, and it is those well-planned steady hours that make a good horse.

When you ride with a trainer, both you and your horse progress. A good trainer will correct your mistakes immediately. He'll have you practice and reinforce efficient, safe ways to ride, and he'll spot your horse's quirks and know how to handle them. I've experienced this progress myself, and I've wondered why I'd done the things that caused trouble when the solution was so simple once someone pointed it out to me. I've helped others with their horses too and seen them progress as a result of my instruction.

Even when the client-horse-trainer relationship works well, you can't spend the rest of your life at it, so you should be prepared to do further schooling at home. That's what the rest of this chapter is about.

Teach your horse his "on the ground" manners

As I've already hinted, teaching, training, or schooling (the three words are nearly synonymous in the horse world) is a complicated business. But for someone who wishes to be a horseman rather than just an owner, it's a necessary and logical step.

The first thing you need to do is picture the kind of behavior you want from your horse. If you're just starting with horses, your picture should be of a quiet, well-mannered, honest pleasure horse, whether you're working with a green colt or a seasoned old-timer (the fact that a horse has thirty or even sixty days with a trainer, by the way, does not qualify him as "seasoned"). The picture should include a light mouth and a good attitude, an animal you can go on with to bigger and better things. Don't picture a horse running a 15-second barrel race or clearing a 5-foot jump. These things come much, much later.

You need to understand too that even the simplest schooling must be broken down into its component parts and those parts presented in a logical, progressive manner. You never ask your horse for a complete maneuver until he knows its component parts well. The only other approach is to rough the horse around, hoping you will stay on and the horse in some mysterious fashion will suddenly find it within himself to accomplish the maneuver you want. But realistically, training just doesn't work this way. Neither will training work if you think you can pet and feed and love your horse into doing the right thing. You must train him in correct behavior, piece by piece, in a pattern his brain can assimilate without anger or fear.

A third thing to remember is that frequent and intelligent use will often overcome the personality flaws that could make your horse unlikable if not handled properly. This is summed up in the old rule: sweat makes good horses. But it has to be intelligent sweat.

While the first three steps of training involve picturing, understanding, and remembering, steps four through infinity involve the actual work. I list here a series of basic training items and some good ways to check a new horse for each of them.

Tying: Any horse when tied should stand quietly for hours, and he should allow you to do any number of reasonable things to him while he is tied. He shouldn't pull back against the rope, shouldn't prance, paw, nip, or kick. Teaching him to stand tied is a good item with which to begin schooling him and yourself.

Tie the horse to a strong post with a strong rope, a strong snap, and a strong halter. Tie at his eye level with no more than two feet of slack. That last instruction is an absolute rule any time you tie a horse. Never tie with bridle reins, weak equipment, or long slack. If you take a double wrap around the post before you tie your halter knot, his pulling back won't jam the knot. Now, pick up his feet, touch his ears, scratch his belly and privates, bump against him, lean on him, reach up between his legs and pull his tail, brush out his tail while standing alongside him. Some horses will put up with all of this, some won't. When you find the things he won't tolerate, do them until he will tolerate them. Don't do anything to hurt him. Don't punish him for jumping around. Just quietly go back to what you were doing until he stands still. This might take a few days of repetition, but it works. Only rarely will a horse have quirks you can't cure. Be careful. Don't surprise him, and don't think he won't kick, bite, or smack you with his head. They all can, and some will.

Suppose he pulls back violently. This is a common trick. It's certainly annoying, and it can be dangerous. Several gimmicks can help break this habit. Try each until you find one that works. Don't leave the horse unattended during the first few sessions with any of these techniques.

Tied high, and that rhymes with **eye**. He's tied short too, which doesn't rhyme with much that makes sense here. But it's the rule anyway. Tie short and at eye level. Also, tie to posts rather than rails. Rails (or planks) will pull off the post if the horse jerks back.

Tied long, and that rhymes with **wrong**.

Tying the halter knot: lead-rope goes around the post from right to left, forming what looks like the figure **4**. Free end is still in right hand. The piece of rope disappearing behind the right wrist goes to the horse.

A half twist of the left hand forms a loop. A sharp bend (bight) is formed in right hand. The bight is run through the loop.

The loop is jammed tight around bight. Pulling on the danglng free end unties the knot.

Detail of the double wrap before tying a halter knot.

Gimmick number one is a "Be Nice" halter, a commercially made product which, as the horse pulls back, threatens to squeeze his brains out his ears. It won't cut, scar, or bruise, but it will hurt, and the instant he quits pulling, it loosens. The beauty of it is that when the horse does the right thing, he rewards himself.

Variations on the "Be Nice" halter include a variety of war-bridles, which can be fashioned from a lariat. A simple one is shown in photos. If you can get the job done another way, however, don't use this. It is very severe, and it doesn't loosen as well as

the "Be Nice" halter. Never use a war-bridle on a young horse.

Gimmick number two uses a stout lariat placed around the belly just behind the front shoulders. Tie a bowline or use a metal honda, because other knots and hondas can jam tight. Run the free end between the front legs and through the tie ring of the halter. Then tie this free end to a post with 2 or 3 feet of slack. Stand back. When a horse pulls against this, the rope around his belly gets uncomfortable fast; most horses will come forward in a rush.

Ol' Gus models the way a good horse wears this nameless gimmick for tying a puller.

93

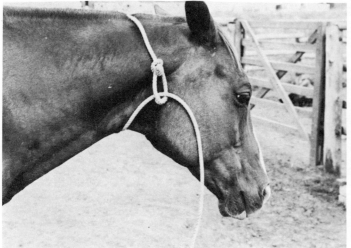

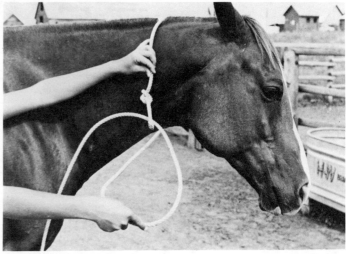

This simple war-bridle is guaranteed to command attention. Step one is just a lariat around the neck with the hondo pointing down on the same side as the handle.

Step two: Put a loop in the rope by making a half-twist.

As with any other gimmick, think ahead. When the horse pulls back, he will tighten the knot around the post; take two wraps to avoid this. He could throw himself and hang from the rope; use a halter knot that can be jerked loose. He could get his feet in the rope; tie short and high. He could fly forward and stick his feet through the fence; tie to something safe, strong, and smooth, such as corner posts or barn walls. Wire fence, steel posts, car bumpers, and clothesline posts just don't qualify.

Gimmick number three is really a schooling trick to use before there is a problem. Run a halter rope through the wall of a corral or barn and tie to an old tire laid on the ground. When the horse backs up, he will pull the tire off the ground. Until the tire hits the wall, this arrangement won't stop him from pulling, but he will get tired (pardon the pun) of pulling against it, and he will learn that stepping ahead releases pressure. I give credit for this trick to a magazine article I've long since lost track of; it's a good idea. Here again the horse rewards himself for correct behavior: the ideal training arrangement.

Number four doesn't really cure problems

either, but it does promote understanding, and it can be used with problem horses or with green horses. Tie your horse in a barn all night for many nights. Feed and water him there, and eventually he will know that being tied is okay. As with other methods, you'll want to check on him until you are confident he isn't doing something bizarre in the night. Think ahead. Make a careful check for any protruding objects. All previous precautions are still in effect.

Once in a while you will end up with a confirmed puller. Sparky was one, a medium-size pony my kids rode for several years. He stood quietly tied to trees or single posts, but blank walls or anything that moved slightly would send him flying back. Once he pulled back while my son Jeff was tying him, and a loop of rope jerked tight around Jeff's hand. Only skin abrasions resulted, but it was a close call. With this kind of problem, you have to avoid the risk whenever you can. If you decide the problem is incurable and you are frightened of the horse, get rid of him.

*Step three: Complete the process by putting the lower loop around the nose. The upper loop should be snugged up close to the ears. Caution: This is a **mean, mean** arrangement. Never leave a horse unattended in it.*

Hobbling: Hobbling may already be part of your horse's schooling if a professional has worked him, but check on it anyway. As with any other new training, start in a strong corral. Be sure nothing in the corral dirt will injure the horse's knees.

There are many good styles of hobbles. For training, I prefer soft "twist hobbles," since anything synthetic can burn skin, and anything with buckles can cut or bruise.

Horses may throw a fit on the first hobbling or two, but they seldom hurt themselves; don't get excited. The way to avoid too much trouble is to put the hobbles on for only a few minutes the first several lessons. Do this two or three times a day for a couple of days, and soon your horse won't fight them at all. He may learn to gallop away in them though, so remember they aren't foolproof. You probably don't want to

Twist hobbles are good for teaching your horse to stand for anything. Place them up on the legs as shown, though almost invariably they'll settle down just above the hooves. These could have been one twist tighter.

Chain hobbles, or grazing hobbles are good for the hobble-broke horse. These allow tiny steps and thus allow quiet grazing in your backyard or out in the wilderness. The pair shown is too big for the pony, and should be pulled a couple of holes tighter.

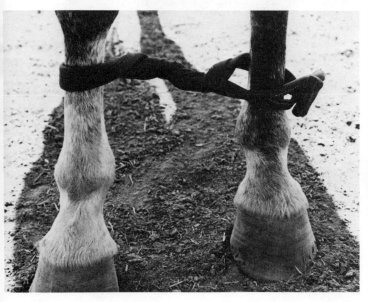

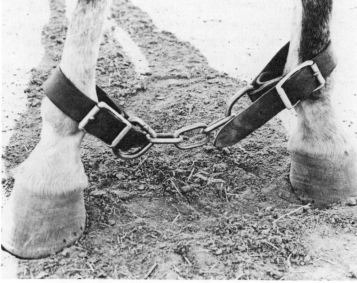

hobble colts less than two years old, since hobbles could injure growing bones.

Along with hobbling front feet, you should practice "scotch hobbling." Use only large diameter cotton rope for this. A good cinch or burlap bag tied around the pastern, as shown in the photos, will reduce the risk of rope burns. Grass or synthetic rope can burn the skin badly.

Tie a loop around the lower part of the neck. Use a bowline only, or you might hang your horse. Run the rope back to a hind foot and fiddle with the horse until you can either pick up the hoof and slip the rope around the pastern, or make him step over the rope. Then bring the rope back to the base of the neck and pull it through the original loop. Pull the foot up about 12 inches off the ground and tie the loose end to the neck loop with a halter knot. The halter knot is again a must so you can quickly undo a wreck. But don't get in a rush to jerk loose. Most horses will at least kick at this arrangement until they figure out that it won't come loose. Some may take many minutes before they fight it at all. If your horse kicks out of this, patiently start again, but put it back on with one extra loop around the pastern.

Restraining a horse with hobbles and halters is sound psychology because it overcomes his natural inclination to run from everything he doesn't understand. When he can't run, he thinks, and sooner or later it dawns on him there is a connection between the rope in your hands and his helplessness. You are communicating that you are the boss hoss.

Use a cinch around the pastern if you don't own cotton rope.

While hobbles and scotch hobbles are often used only on green horses, they are also good for well-broke horses. There will be times when you must doctor a sore leg, and the horse won't allow you to do so. Hobble him and scotch hobble the sound leg; you can doctor all you want if the horse is accustomed to restraint. There may come a time when you want to put on a load the horse doesn't like. Scotch hobble him. You may have to tie up in a strange place. Hobble the horse, and he won't paw the ground all night. You may need to restrain him at shoeing time. Hobbles and scotch hobbles will help.

Once you are confident the horse will stand tied and hobbled you are past another potential problem: the horse that prances around when you are trying to saddle him. He is also much safer when other people are around because he is less apt to leap on top of them just for laughs. You can stop during a ride and go to the bathroom when you need to. You can even tie up to a tree without having it pawed out by the roots when you return.

Longeing: Longeing is the technique of working a horse in circles at the end of a long rope or webbing lead. There are many levels of schooling that can be accomplished with longeing, but the backyard horseman will most frequently use it as a tool to calm a nervous horse and to make a reluctant horse begin obeying. Many people use it as part of a breaking routine, then forget it as the horse progresses. But longeing should be repeated from time to time just for discipline.

Starting a horse longeing often seems difficult until you learn that success is mainly a matter of where you stand in relation to the horse's body. If you step into the direction of his travel, he tries to stop or turn away. But if you maintain a position more toward his rear end, he will think you are chasing him and will continue to move ahead.

Start by using a regular halter rope in one hand and a stock whip (or maybe an old fishing rod) in the other. Step back toward his rump and away from his body perhaps 3 feet, and tap him on the tail or lower legs with the whip; at the same time, command "walk." He may step away from you instead of ahead, and in that case you must move toward his rump and try again. Some horses will start right out while others just turn to face you. You have to be patient. Keep at the job from both sides until the horse circles freely at the end of the halter rope. With many horses a crude longeing job can be accomplished in the first five minutes. Try it two or three times a day for a couple of days, and you will get beyond the accidental stage and into the learned stage. As soon as the longeing is working at all,

No self-respecting horse will voluntarily walk through old truck tires, but, if there is a longe line involved, one has to do what one has to do.

increase your line to about 20 feet.

Once the horse longes freely, teach him an absolute "whoa" by stepping toward his direction of travel, as if you were heading him off; at the same time, shout "whoa." You may have to wave the whip in his face to get his attention, but don't do this so much that he starts throwing his head. Teaching him this voice command from the ground is a great help later when you are riding. You can also teach him to discriminate between "walk," "trot," "canter," and "whoa," if you take your time.

The most practical use comes as you gradually put down small logs, sheets of plastic, rows of old tires, and longe him through it all. You'll have him doing absolutely what you tell him to, and you'll seldom have to do more than wave the whip or slap the ground with it. After one or two quick little snaps in early lessons, he will respect but not fear it. If you delight in hearing the smack of whip on flesh, you will soon have a battle on your hands. can be even more completely "bomb-proofed." Start by putting a couple of small stones in two plastic milk jugs. Tie the jugs together with about 5 feet of baler twine with a 6-inch loop in the middle of the twine. Hang one jug on either side of the horse with the loop over the saddle horn. Now longe him. When he can stand this

kind of rattling, he's a better horse. Do the same with a feed sack on each end of the twine instead of, or in addition to, the milk jugs. Put a slicker or piece of plastic over the entire horse, and longe him some more. This will save trouble when you need to ride wearing a slicker.

You can take longeing even further. Longe with a rope dragging from the saddle horn. Eventually add a feed sack, a stick of wood, an old tire, again taking a week or more for this amount of training. You'll have a horse that isn't going to panic if you need to lead another horse or drag camp wood or try your hand at roping.

All of these things improve the horse's manners without endangering you and without taking a lot of time or money. Remember, do them in a strong corral, and introduce them a little at a time.

Many writers explain these longeing techniques as part of the breaking process. I'm suggesting them here as things that should be done with older horses too until they are accustomed to almost anything. I also pass them on as things you do a little at a time, taking perhaps a week or more to get through the amount of longeing I've just described and reinforcing with an occasional lesson every year. Though you can start longeing a yearling or two-year-old, and though this will begin teaching mental discipline, you can overdo longeing

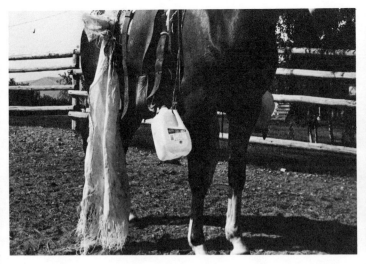

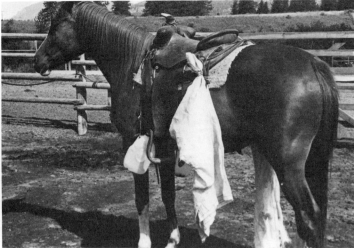

There are stones rattling in the milk jugs, and the sacks rustle in the breeze. But after a few hours it's all old hat.

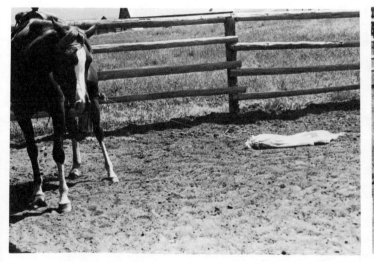

The sack has many uses. This is one of the scarier ones.

But in a little while it, too, is soon just another minor annoyance.

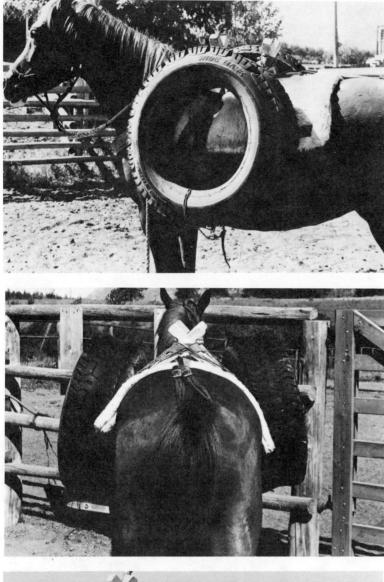

Two views of the ol' tire-packin' trick. Do it in a good corral, and do it after plenty of other bomb-proofing work.

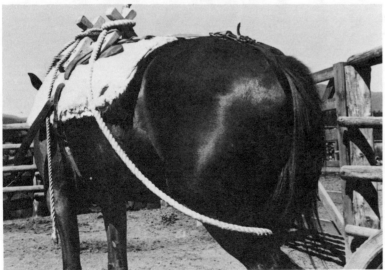

One way to get a horse over his foolishness about ropes under the tail. A couple hours of this today. Tomorrow the rope is raised for a couple of hours. Next day it's up in the private zone. Note that this mare is already over her silliness: she wears a crupper without a fuss.

When a horse loads so well that you only have to step out of his way, that's manners.

with young horses. Growing bones can be damaged by the constant tight circling. Give the lessons, but don't just longe for the sake of longeing.

Driving: Once the horse has been longeing for a while and you've done some bomb-proofing, teach him to drive. A mature horse may already know this, but driving has uses beyond breaking, just as longeing does, so you may want to practice it anyway.

After a few minutes of longeing, stop and clip long lines to the halter, or to a hackamore, caveson, or snaffle bit. Two longe straps will do nicely as lines. Run these back through the stirrups, one on each side. Tie the stirrups down to the cinch with a short string for this training, but don't forget that you've done so. Another trick is to tie a piece of inner-tubing between lines and snaffle bit to absorb shock.

Now step back and begin longeing again, using the inside line as your longe line. While the horse is circling, begin tightening the circle by pulling the inside rein with light tugs, never long, steady pulls. When the horse moves at a walk, tug the opposite line and turn him around the other way. When he is moving straight ahead, stop him with voice commands and alternating tugs. Teach him to back up with alternating tugs and the command "back." Expect only a

step or two for the first few tries. Be patient, calm, and gentle. Once you are confident the horse is responding out of understanding more than out of luck, take him into a bigger arena or pasture and drive some more.

Driving teaches control, and it can have uses in later training. Suppose you wish to train for pulling a buggy or cutter or simply pulling your kids on a toboggan. If you can drive the horse, you can pull light objects in the corral, and you are still out of the way of danger. For pulling practice, driving is naturally more practical than longeing because it gives you control of the same sort and from the same position as when you're actually pulling an object. After some of this practice, your first trips with a buggy will be a lot safer than if you'd just hooked up and taken off.

Suppose you wish to sharpen up your horse after a long winter off. Longe him, drive him, and without getting on his back, you've reinforced the fact that you're in command. Suppose you just want to loosen up his neck and make him give his head to you more freely. Driving, done carefully and quietly, will help a great deal.

Loading: None of the training mentioned so far may seem important if your picture of horsemanship is a wild gallop into the sunset. But if you wish to have a quiet,

A cheap and safe way to teach your horse to load: the trailer is securely positioned in a small corral. Put the food and water inside, and sooner or later, the problem solves itself.

well-mannered horse that will neither hurt nor embarrass you—and you should be wishing this—these techniques will be very helpful. Besides, they're fun to try, and they're simple enough that the novice will gain some confidence for later training. They're also cost-free, and they'll give you a clearer understanding of what personality type you're working with, something well worth knowing about your horse.

But, you aren't done yet with ground manners. Your horse should load and unload easily from any vehicle. If you bought a used horse, he probably already does. But if he doesn't load, here are some techniques you can try. Before you begin, check all equipment for strength and for anything on your truck or trailer that could cut, bruise, stab, or otherwise mutilate you or the horse.

Let's begin with loading into a pickup. Be sure it has a wooden floor or rubber mats over the metal floor.

Back the pickup up to a bank or ramp that will allow a flat walk-in. Be sure there are no gaps for horse hooves to slip into. Start by quietly and confidently leading right up to and into the rack. Pretend that nothing could possibly go wrong, and about half the time nothing will. If the horse wants to stop and smell things, let him. Be patient, and start again with gentle tugs. There is no use trying to drag him in. You just aren't strong enough.

If the horse is hesitant, have an assistant pat him on the rump and loudly question his—the horse's—intelligence or ancestry. Often this little encouragement will get the horse moving. If the horse loads, reward him with grain or cubes.

Sometimes a horse just needs time. If he paws the rack, if he sniffs the floor, if he makes false starts but doesn't quite jump in, these are good indications that he will cooperate; but he just has to worry for a while yet.

With some horses, much more discussion is necessary. You may be able to lure some recalcitrant loaders with grain, but it has been my experience that if the horse balks at loading, luring won't work. Most of the time, one of the following tricks will.

If you are alone, loop a lariat around the horse's rump and take the free end of the lariat into the rack with you. Alternately tug on the halter and the lariat. Be careful. Some horses will feel that rope and leap in on top of you. If you have help, let the people outside the rack tug the rope up against the horse's rump. A related trick is to put the lariat around the horse's belly as explained earlier for pullers.

If the horse becomes sullen, fights his way around to the side of the truck, or sits back against all ropes and refuses to budge, you may have to take more drastic steps. Sometimes a longe-broke horse can be forced in by lining him up with the back and

The technique described in the text to teach loading can be adapted to training your horse to negotiate all sorts of obstacles. Here a young filly learns to cross a "bridge." Early one morning a bridge appears between the pen with water and the pen with hay. It's a frightening sight, folks.

But by the next morning, this little filly will cross a dozen times a day.

giving him a sharp smack with the whip. But this is a questionable practice, since he may go in, but he may also go crazy and still not load.

Another, more extreme trick is to tie a lariat to the halter, run the free end around a bar at the front of the rack and bring it out the back alongside the horse. Continue around the horse's rump and through a bar on the opposite side of the rack, but on the back wall. You have tied the horse into position. Now stir him up with a slap or yell, and take the slack out of the rope each time he moves. You will be forcing him in because he has no other place to go. This is a last-resort method, dangerous for you, the horse, and the rack or trailer.

Frequently a problem with loading is that we don't try to load a horse until we need to, and then we find he won't load. A better method than any so far is to train the horse to load long before you're desperate. Don't be fooled by the fact that somebody got the horse to your home. There may have been a real battle or even a handful of tranquilizers.

A method that uses time instead of force is to park your vehicle in a position where the horse can get in by himself, and leave the vehicle there for a few days. Be sure it can't move up, down, forward, or backward. Then shut off the water and food supply except for what you leave in plain sight in the vehicle. Let the horse train himself to load and unload. It works, it's painless, and it's permanent. Be patient. The horse may grow pretty hungry before he cooperates.

A customer once brought me a range colt in a stock truck. The owner had dragged the colt aboard with a saddle horse. The colt was as reluctant to unload as she had been to load. I put hay and water at the bottom of the ramp and left. It took nearly a day for the filly to come down. When she did, I let her drink a gallon of water and take a bite of hay. Then I moved both items back up into the truck. By the next day she was jogging up and down the ramp for entertainment.

Cruel? I don't think so. Before I tried this method, both the owner and I were being pretty rough on this filly and getting nothing out of it except anger, which could have made things even worse.

The loading methods described here work basically the same for truck, trailer, or pickup. If you reinforce good behavior and if you think far enough ahead to prevent injury, most horses will soon load cheerfully simply by being led to the opening and having the halter rope tossed over their shoulders as they step in. Most will soon back out carefully if you tug on their tails or turn and step out if they're in trucks or wide trailers. I've found it handy with pickups to gradually load from a lower and lower surface. Soon the horse will jump into any pickup from the road surface if he never

lands on a slippery floor and if he gets an occasional handful of grain for reinforcement. It is also handy with pickups to teach the horse to turn and jump down as well as back out.

Even with well-trained horses, accidents can happen while loading. Even the gentlest horses sometimes panic, and they will kick, strike, stomp on you, or beat you senseless with their thrashing heads. Never be inside a vehicle in a position that you can't escape from. If you're in a dangerous situation, don't hesitate: scoot up over the top or out the escape door.

An experienced horseman who lives near me, unloading a well-broke, experienced cow horse, stood helpless when the horse put one hind leg under the trailer too far, sat down, flipped over backwards, and smashed his head on the ground. That horse never stood up again; he died in a matter of minutes. Absolutely nothing was done wrong by the humans involved.

The same day that horseman told me about losing his horse, I unloaded several horses from my stock truck and carelessly left a 4-inch gap between truck and ramp. One horse stuck his leg into that gap to the knee. I knew as I watched it happen there was nothing I could do to prevent a broken leg, particularly since I was behind the horse instead of leading him out as I should have been. This time, however, I was lucky.

The horse pulled his leg out and continued down without a scratch.

Carelessness breeds disaster, but sometimes disasters happen even when we've done our best. My neighbor-horseman has only his loss to mourn; I would have had to mourn my carelessness as well.

Teach your horse his manners from the saddle.

So far you've either taught or proved your horse's good manners while he's standing tied, longeing, driving, and loading. Assuming you've done some riding along the way, you should be pretty well acquainted with him by now. But there is still more he should know.

Mounting: Well-schooled horses stand still while you mount and for as long as it takes to adjust yourself in the saddle. Teaching the horse to stand for mounting is much easier if you have already taught him to stand restrained. Now you can put those hobbles or scotch hobbles to real use. Tie and hobble him and mount a dozen times on each side. Do this several days in a row with either a bad-mannered horse or a green one, and he will begin to understand what you want. As soon as you've done the trick with

him restrained, mount with him standing free. When he stands quietly, reward him by going on to something else. One precaution: don't jam your foot clear into the stirrup while mounting, since you could get hung up. Another precaution: leave a hobbled horse tied for mounting practice. A hobbled horse who isn't tied can run off and dump himself with you underneath.

Each time you mount, give the "whoa" command and demand absolute obedience. Demanding doesn't mean violence. It means firm voice commands, light tugs on the reins, and patience enough not to mount until the horse is still.

If the horse won't stand unless hobbled even after your best efforts, try this old cowboy trick. Hobble him by twisting a halter rope around his forelegs and tying it with a halter knot. Take the free end up into the saddle with you, and pull it loose from there. You'll have to keep your wits about you, since the knot you tie will determine whether you are mounted on a hobbled horse or one you can turn loose.

Riding: You're mounted. How should a well-mannered horse act while you're riding?

First, he doesn't move until you're ready, and when you ask, the lightest of signals brings a response. He will walk smartly, at least after he loosens up, and you won't have to spur him along to keep that walk going.

A well-mannered horse won't panic, not if a rainstorm breaks and you need your slicker, not if a truck or a train bears down on you from behind. Once I was caught with three horses between railroad tracks and a high dirt bank. Naturally a train came along, a hundred roaring freight cars 30 feet away and 10 feet above us. The horses danced a little and rolled their eyes, but none of them panicked. I didn't breathe the whole time. But these horses live within a hundred yards of a track, and they see trains daily.

A well-mannered horse won't go into a tizzy every time he sees a new horse. He's attentive to your signals even if he isn't trained to do everything. A well-mannered horse will put in a hard day for you without complaint. In fact, he'll husband his strength, avoid fidgeting, and stand still when you stop for a rest. He'll also try new things without fighting them. If you back him into a roping box for the first time, he may not know what you'll do next, and he may be nervous, but he won't throw a fit. A well-mannered horse may stumble over the cavalettis and hesitate at the first jump, but he won't shy, buck, or run away.

How does your horse attain this well-mannered state?

Through experience naturally. And how do you get all this experience without the horse doing some silly things? Is this Catch-22? Not exactly. Of course you'll have trouble before you can call your horse well-mannered, and even when your horse has all the experience you can give him, he'll continue to annoy you at times. This is just a normal part of using a horse.

As much as possible, experience must come under controlled circumstances. This can make the difference between annoyance and disaster. Much of your early riding should be done with manners in mind, not major events or activities. Take the horse out near the highway or railroad and stand there insisting calmly on obedience. Take him to unfamiliar horses frequently, but in ways that won't interfere with others' business. Set up minor obstacles for him at home and change his surroundings often, even if you only hang a tarp next to his water tank. Ride him to and through things he doesn't like often enough to make him forget his silliness. These may not be enjoyable rides, but they don't have to be long. They certainly will be valuable.

All of this takes time—slowly adding the new and repeating the old over dozens of sessions, getting results and having setbacks, going at it again. The younger the horse you buy, the more of this kind of riding you'll need. Don't start resenting this time. It's part of what you volunteered for when you decided "to get into horses," and both you and the horse will be learning things.

Here's an example of what can happen if you don't do this kind of schooling. An acquaintance was competing at state-level jumping on an exceptionally able gelding, which always traveled with his dam, another good jumper. The gelding had the habit of spinning back somewhere on the course and heading toward wherever his dam stood waiting the turn. No amount of strength or skill could stop him once he turned, and no amount of guesswork could predict on which course or which day he would or wouldn't turn. At the state show he dumped my acquaintance, ruining both her performance and her peace of mind.

This kind of habit must be cured, and a few months away from the dam would at least begin the job. The extra time, even if not specifically jumping time, would in the long run improve this horse's performance ability, since it would end the kind of annoying and dangerous habit the horse has become known for.

Time and again people have told me, "I'd love to go along, but I've never loaded my horses," or "He won't stand tied, so I won't be able to bring him," or "She's in heat so I don't know if I should use her," or "He won't go away from other horses. What do I do?"

My reaction is: "If you can't get the most basic performance out of your horses, why have them at all?"

Such dilemmas illustrate again why professionals are often skeptical of back-yard owners. Professionals take the need for basic performance and manners as a matter of course. Such dilemmas also illustrate the difference between an owner and a horseman. An owner will dump a horse into events he isn't ready for, making an ass of himself and a nervous wreck of the horse; a horseman builds piece by piece, starting with sound foundations. Even when the work isn't completely polished, the horseman and his horse will have class, or quality, while the mere owner will be a jamming, cursing, spurring, rationalizing embarrassment to the horse world.

Train your hands and legs

If you are male, chances are you're proud of your strength. But mounted and riding, your strength can be a hindrance, because a good rider must become light-handed, almost limp-wristed. A primitive school of horse training believes it takes strength to hold a horse, and while this is true in rough-and-tumble situations, strength doesn't teach a horse to obey. Strength attacking a horse's mouth teaches him to fight. The biggest, meanest bit in the world

Legs and hands: your gas pedal, steering wheel, brakes, and shifting mechanism. Learn to use them in complex and delicate harmomy.

Hands low, and the pinky finger suggests a turn.

won't stop the horse that hasn't been schooled to stop. Making every turn a surprise wherein you jerk the horse's head clear around to your knee won't teach a fast or controlled turn.

Being light-handed is especially necessary with young horses to avoid bad habits and tough mouths. Learn to hint with the reins, not demand.

Related to the business of light hands is the use of light bits, not light in weight but light in terms of severity. The plain snaffle used properly (adjusted just tight enough to make a light wrinkle in the corners of the mouth) will serve for many training purposes if you stay light-handed. You don't need to "start" young horses with harsh bits from some misguided fear of runaways or buckers. You start a horse in the snaffle to keep his mouth light. Better yet you do basic arena training in a hackamore or caveson. Teach him what you can without any metal-to-mouth pressure, and he'll be a better horse for it.

Your legs are the second major method of communication. They push and bump to move the rear half of the horse forward, back, left, and right. When you learn to lightly coordinate hands and legs to put the horse exactly where you want him, you move into a whole new dimension of riding.

108

Know where you're going

Just as you would when training for manners, you can break down any specific event and train for it in pieces. In fact, you must do it that way. A professional trainer can take you step-by-step toward a goal even if you have only the vaguest idea of that goal, because the trainer has the pieces clearly in mind. But for many backyard horsemen a trainer is out of the question. That's where the good training books come into play. They have the breaking-into-pieces done for you. Read them until they stay in your memory, until you can feel through the seat of your saddle and the reins in your hands: "that's what that writer was talking about!" It may take a month or two to get your horse simply to give his neck muscles and turn lightly toward you, but if you understand this as part of a sequence heading toward a goal, you won't mind. Think of the ugly alternatives: the rushing along, an unruly horse, starting over, or maybe the search for a new horse.

Understand and employ the processes of psychological conditioning

Nearly everyone has heard of the psychologist Pavlov's drooling dog. Pavlov "taught" a dog to salivate by turning on a light, then feeding the dog. When the dog came to associate the stimulus (light) with the positive reinforcement (food), Pavlov could elicit a response (drooling) simply by turning on the light. Pavlov's was the first scientific description of classical conditioning, a thoroughly practical phenomenon for anyone schooling horses to understand.

Conditioning theory says that if a stimulus (cue or signal) is given and the right response follows, and if that response is followed with a reward, learning will take place. This is conditioning using positive reinforcement. Horses and other animals can also be taught by setting up unpleasant situations, which they can avoid with the correct behavior. This is conditioning using negative reinforcement. It is also called aversive conditioning. In simple terms, we are talking about the carefully planned use of rewards and punishment.

While humans can put off the reward because we can enjoy the anticipation, animals cannot. It's sometimes possible to bribe good behavior out of the kids in the back seat even if they have to wait a while

An example of the small steps that go into teaching a horse to turn. A chunk of baling twine makes a cheap and expendable bitting rig when tied to the stirrup. This filly shows by her facial expressions that she doesn't like the gimmick and isn't accustomed to it. But, she will learn. She rewards herself when she yields to the light pressure from the weight of the stirrup.

for the hamburgers, but a horse can't make the connection between his quick stop at 4 o'clock and an extra bite of oats at 8. Nor can he make the connection between his nip on your shoulder yesterday and the slap you give his nose today. He can't understand even timely punishment if it is so severe it rattles his brain. If he nips, an immediate slap on the nose is perfectly clear to him and perfectly justifiable in psychological terms. But a 5-minute lapse while you find a stick followed by a dozen blows with the stick, don't make sense to him. You have now given him a new stimulus—pain—and he will use his fear reaction against you in some way.

Look for ways to use positive reinforcement, rewards, because they are more effective than negative reinforcement in training. Grain can be a good reward, but it can also lead to disrespect if the horse begins to see you only as a provider of grain. More practical rewards are the pat on the neck, the scratching of the chest, the immediate release of pressure on rope or bit.

Think about conditioning in terms of a particular training broken down into its smallest parts. We want a good fast rein, but the first tiny steps involve only placing the horse's head or feet with the reins. So we tug lightly, and if the head moves in the right direction, we relax the pressure: stimulus, response, positive reinforcement. As each tiny move is practiced and learned, we ask for a little more. The original stimulus brings an increasingly complex response, but the reinforcement remains the same. That's the psychology behind the "knowing where you're going" principle, and it's the mental muscle behind all the little sequences professional trainers use. You can use it too, if you know how it works and apply it logically.

I hope I've convinced you that horsemanship includes a lot of basic training for you and your horse and that basic training is just as important as the fine tuning that comes later. Work, work, work, on these basics, and read, read, read about these and more specific subjects. There is no shortage of good information.

A SET OF REASONABLE EXPECTATIONS FOR HORSES OF VARIOUS AGES

Two-year-old
    Trailer loading
    Standing tied quietly
    Being handled while tied, including feet; one set shoes if necessary for schooling
    Longe at walk, trot
    Voice commands while longeing: walk, trot, whoa, back
    Being led behind broke horses; this to gain outside experience
    Saddling, bridling, longeing with tack, blankets, slickers, etc.
    Riding
        Walk, trot, definite stop, a few slow canters in arena
        Standing for mounting, standing up to two minutes during schooling
        Light or willing response to direct rein
        Backing four or five steps smoothly
        Quiet but aggressive walk on pleasure rides, up to two hours
        During pleasure rides, becoming familiar with traffic, bridges, dogs, etc., preferably under controlled circumstances
    Note: actual riding time is two months or less of steady work. After that, occasional reinforcement, perhaps a week at a time three or four times through late summer and fall. Lightweight riders only.

Three-year-old
    Review of previous training, plus:
    Hobbles, scotch hobbles
    Regular, careful shoeing
    Full season of light, controlled work, which can include travel to shows, trail rides, for outside experience
    No strenuous work such as roping, jumping
    Schooling for taking leads on command, some collection, neck-reining for general riding. Schooling can go on steadily for up to two months. Hard, sliding stops should be avoided, though basic training for this and other more strenuous work can begin. Cavalettis, light-weight pulling or packing are good. Manners still more important than event training.

Four-year-old
    Review of previous training, plus:
    Basic training in specific events, but not endurance riding. Roping could include box training, running stock, roping small calves on soft surface. Jumping could include cavalettis, technique, low jumps. Dressage could include basic-level training over extended time.
    Plenty of pleasure riding, all-day trips, pack trips; long, slow work is still preferable to short, fast work. Can work full season of slow work, even with full loads.

Five-year-old
    Review of previous training, plus:
    Serious competition training—including short endurance competition; "hot" events such as gymkhana, barrel-racing, roping, polo, should still be interspersed often with quiet work.

MISCELLANEOUS DISPOSITION CHARACTERISTICS
(subject to many variations)

Two-year-old

Much silly behavior, unpredictability, moodiness, flight-instinct very strong, curiosity very strong. Give up mentally very quickly under heavy work.

Three-year-old

Often similar to two-year-old; mentally more stable but still frequently inattentive; will still give up mentally under heavy use.

Four-year-old

If green, expect resistance. Panic or anger reaction is more dangerous because of greater strength and coordination.

If schooled for some time, stable mentally, still capable of much more silliness than older horse, but usually predictable. Will not give up mentally nearly as soon as younger horses. Still not to be confused dispositionally with a mature, well-schooled horse, and not to be trusted as such.

chapter nine
Getting In On The Action

In the winter, cabin fever simmers at the edge of my consciousness all the time—not because I have nothing to do, you understand, but because there is so little horseback activity. I've been this way since I was a kid, and I'm not sure why. It is evidence, though, of the difference between two groups of horsemen: the performance-oriented, and the production-oriented. I belong in the former. I'm not happy just raising horses or looking at them, though I've enjoyed the colts I've had. I've just got to be doing something active with horses, and I firmly believe that doing is what moves dead-end horses and riders off center.

Pleasure riding

Pleasure riding is just what it sounds like—riding for enjoyment. It encompasses afternoon ambles in the countryside around your home and work in your arena. It's the activity most beginners begin with and probably the most common recreational use of horses. Pleasure riding attracts all sorts of riders: young and old, rich and poor, lazy and ambitious. Pleasure riding is simple, but it isn't just a matter of climbing aboard any available horse.

If you're fighting your horse or frightened throughout the whole experience, pleasure riding may be no pleasure at all.

Your horse's manners, which I discussed in the previous chapter, will make or break your pleasure riding. And when your horse's manners are good, pleasure riding won't dead-end with ambling up the same old road. You can teach maneuvers like the side-pass, cantering on correct leads, quick stops, and many other skills whether you ride English or western. You can continue to learn new things and refine the old, all under the heading of pleasure riding, and you can do much of it in your own back yard.

Good pleasure horses provide transportation too if you decide to head into the back country. Like other activities, back country travel isn't as simple as it appears, and a good pack/camping trip requires much preparation. Start simple, read a few good books, and practice what they preach. Joe Back's *Horses, Hitches, and Rocky Trails* is a minor classic on the subject and fun to read. Better for the small-party packer is Elser and Brown's *Packin' In On Mules and Horses*.

Of course, many people sooner or later feel motivated to test themselves in competition. Pleasure classes provide an excellent way to do this because there are so many levels of competition. Naturally, the top levels are dominated by the top professionals. If they've made a reputation and a living from an event, they must be good at it. But a dedicated backyarder, given time, motivation, and the right horse, can compete even at the top levels in this event more readily than in many others.

If you try group trail-riding, remember these simple rules:

Never pass the leader.
Don't run your horse.
Ride single-file. Pass others only when necessary.
Tie a red ribbon on the tail of a horse that kicks.
Leave your dogs, stallions, and very young children at home.
At stops, tend horses before yourself.
Tie horses away from each other to avoid fights.
If a rider needs to stop, always have another rider or two stop with him or her.

Roping

Roping is fast, rugged, and complex, a worthwhile goal for any horseman, male or female, and it's accessible to the backyard horseman. Good ropers and good roping horses are made over a long period. Ropers spend hundreds of hours practicing on the ground and in the saddle. They spend months training horses to stand in the box, run up on steer or calf, hold position, turn and stop hard, and work the rope on command. Few ropers ever profit from the event when you account for the investment in horses, training, equipment, transportation, practice and entry fees. The pay-off is in the moment of satisfaction when your loop lands right and your horse is working well.

You can't go far in roping if there is no one else locally interested. Fortunately, almost anywhere there are horses and cattle, there is roping. You also need a good arena, chutes, and a steady supply of replacement cattle. Many people meet these needs through a club or a similar organization.

Any reasonably intelligent and willing horse can learn roping, but because it is such a strenuous event, physical more than mental attributes separate good rope horses from poor ones most of the time. A fine-boned horse, one with serious old injuries, or one with serious faults in build or movement can be used for many things, but roping is not among them. You need strong, sound, fast horses for this event.

Roping also is the one event that absolutely requires heavy-duty stock saddles with guaranteed trees and the very best of other gear as well.

Charles O. Williamson's book discusses basic rope-training, but there are others more specialized. *Western Horseman* magazine publishes two: one by calf roper Roy Cooper, the other by team roper Leo Camarillo. Almost no one, however, can learn to rope by reading. Books can help you hone the skills you learn from other ropers, and you must practice, practice, practice.

Cutting

Cutting is among the fastest, most complex, strenuous, and beautiful events in the horse world. While roping is accessible to backyard horsemen, cutting usually isn't. Cutting horses are among the most expensive performance horses in the world, ranking up there with race horses. Facilities for training aren't any more extensive than for roping, but what sets cutting apart in addition to the cost is the level of competition. Even at a novice cutting event there isn't such a thing as a bunch of good ol' boys from down the lane getting together as there is in roping.

Reining

Competitive reining, which includes sliding stops, spectacular spins, rollbacks, flying lead-changes, all done at speed, is perhaps as complex as anything except dressage, and while the competition is fierce, the event is accessible to the backyard horseman in at least one respect—it can be trained for at home with a minimum facility. A beginner, however, will have trouble progressing because the event is so complicated and requires skillful riding. So much of it is usable schooling for any western horse that it is worth pursuing anyway.

Nearly any healthy, sound horse can benefit from and progress in reined training, but for serious competition, the right build and the right personality are

A short, stocky appy mare learns the discipline of jumping while her rider learns the techniques. This mare does well in western equitation classes at 4-H horse shows, and is a reliable trail horse. She will never be more than an adequate jumper, but at age 17, she is exactly what the novice rider should be willing to pay good money for.

both highly important. A horse prone to blow up in anger at every new move will be difficult to work with. You need either a "good horse" or a good "nervous performer" with considerable muscle, good coordination, and good legs. While quarter horses dominate the event—and should, since this is the kind of thing at least some bloodlines were developed for—there are excellent Morgan, appy, and Arab reining horses and contests in addition to open classes.

Serious reined training is not for young horses. While the professionals are often caught in a time and money vice, which makes them train three-year-olds heavily, you don't want to do this since the chances of injury are high with young horses. Also, you'll want to continue other types of uses, pleasure riding for example, to keep the reined horse's mind fresh. A steady dose of reined training with no breaks in the routine will give you a sour horse in most cases.

Jumping

Here in western Montana a common notion of a good horse is one that will pack an elk. Above that is a horse that can survive a long day digging cattle out of the brush. Higher still in this hierarchy is a well-trained rope horse. But it is a measure of the popularity of jumping events, which smack of something eastern or English, that there are many hunters and jumpers right here among the "real" Montana horses.

Jumping, as I will use the term, (which includes "hunting") is quite accessible to the backyard horseman. One reason is that many kinds of horses make good jumpers. The horse must be strong and healthy, willing, and sensible. Height is often an advantage, but at the level of local competition he doesn't need the exceptional coordination of the cutting or reining horse, nor must he tolerate the extreme stress of roping events. Of course at the national level, horses are bred strictly for jumping, and they are both superior and expensive, but at the national level jumping approaches a full-time occupation.

Jumping takes skill and guts. The likelihood of jumping without falling occasionally is low, and the picket fences, for example, will have you pretty nervous on your way down. Perhaps it is the risk as much as the skill that people like.

For equipment you will need a good jumping saddle, a helmet, and a pair of tall English-style riding boots. Western tack is out of the question: the helmet is common sense, and the boots will keep English stirrup leathers from biting big bruises in the calves of your legs. I, of course, not wanting to give the other side any credit, took a few jumping lessons wearing my

12-inch Western boots. It took weeks for the bruises to heal. You'll also need the proper ("correct") clothing for competition. This requirement may sometimes seem impractical, but is no different than many western events where you can be disqualified for the wrong clothing.

Jump training under good instructors is excellent discipline for any horse. You'll be walking, trotting, cantering, changing leads, teaching collection, backing, turning, working over low rails called cavaletti, jumping a variety of obstacles, and just standing in line. You'll see improvement in your horse's manners if nothing else, and the cost will be justified by that alone.

You probably cannot make much progress jumping on your own at home, at least until you are years into the event. Fortunately, in many places you can take lessons on well-schooled horses, build your confidence and skills, and eventually practice at home on your own horse. You can also haul your own horse to lessons.

To the uninitiated, jumping seems to consist only of shoving a horse at an obstacle fast enough that he can't help but leap over. In reality jumping is nearly as complex as an event can get; the good riders and horses merely make it look easy.

Jumping is not a single activity. Jumping embraces many categories and related activities like hunt-seat equitation, hunter-jumper classes, and more—enough variety to give you a lifetime of riding and learning.

Eventing

Since all competitive riding takes place in events, the word "eventing" is confusing. It and the term "three-day" refer to a specific event—a show, spanning three days, in which each horse competes in dressage, stadium jumping, and cross-country jumping. Training is done in many places; the actual event is held at a specially-designed facility. It is a measure of the popularity of this complex and strenuous event that there are two such facilities within easy driving distance of my own small town.

Possibly the best description of eventing can be found in *The USCTA Book of Eventing*, edited by Sally O'Connor, (Addison-Wesley Publishing Company, Inc., 1982). This is an exceptionally well-done book with readable text, many illustrations, good photos, and training schedules.

Eventing is not for timid riders nor is it for silly horses. It aims toward the toughest combination of hard work and complex training any horse and rider can get involved in. It's nonetheless accessible to backyard horsemen at least in its early stages of training. Also at early levels event training doesn't require a super-horse. The training itself will insure that if your horse is any good at all, he'll get better and better. For the serious horseman who has time to invest, eventing can be one of the most rewarding pursuits in the horse world.

As with other English events, equipment needs are not extensive. Basic tack and clothing will get you started, while correct costumes are required for competition.

With both eventing and jumping, you will still have a good pleasure horse after much specialized training. In fact, pleasure riding, English or western, is a good refresher for these horses.

Driving

Driving horses takes a particular kind of space, and this may be one reason its appeal is limited. Whether you're driving in buggy or sleigh, you can't do it on the freeway, on narrow trails, or in heavy traffic; yet it requires space much larger than your arena.

If you do have the space, driving is desirable for many reasons, including the fact that it's just plain fun. It makes better horses out of good ones, even your ropers or jumpers, because it gives them variety and exercise while teaching discipline and manners. Particularly good is the winter

exercise possibility.

While driving does require some skill and sensitive communication with the horse, driving for pleasure isn't complicated. Any tractable horse can be trained for it. As in other training you must progress slowly and in a well-planned sequence to avoid trouble. You'll do a lot of groundwork before you actually get to go for a long, quiet drive. Slow, methodical progress is especially important when you consider how much weight to pull. If you overload green horses, they will either balk or become scared, and you can ruin them in a couple of lessons.

My dad's methods never failed him, but I offer them as an interesting story rather than as something a beginner should try. On a winter morning he would take two well-broke saddle horses, throw on the harness for the first time, hook up to a bobsled, and slap horse rumps with the lines. His first pass around the pasture was spectacular with horses plunging, snow flying in clouds, and Dad standing straight up, handling the lines just enough to keep the horses circling. Eventually the horses slowed, and he moved them out onto the snow-packed roads. When he came back from somewhere, they were pretty well harness broke. Well, Dad at least could drive them. He never hurt the horses and was never in a real wreck, but this may have

Tremendous power and a sweet disposition are trademarks of these Belgians. However, in most cases we backyard horsemen can't do these horses justice.

had something to do with the fact that the early years of his life were spent driving in the hay fields.

A light pulling harness is less expensive than a good saddle, while a heavy harness may cost $500 or more per horse. With reasonable care, a harness will last longer than you will, however. There are companies that specialize in harness and buggy equipment; they advertise in most horse magazines.

For some people pulling can become more of a passion than driving. I've been using the two words interchangeably. The basics are the same, but pulling really means getting serious with heavy loads. For this, heavier horses are necessary even in the lightweight divisions. Pulling, whether for contests or work, is exciting to watch or participate in. You can almost hear well-trained pulling horses thinking "There ain't no way that ton of dead weight can stop me."

Owning heavier horses means more expense in feed, less comfort and athletic ability as saddle horses. Raising these heavies in a backyard operation isn't very practical. However, ownership does offer the advantage of a relatively steady market value. As I write this, saddle horses that could have sold for $1,000 or more a few years ago are unsaleable at half that price, while heavies are holding their value.

Games on horseback

There are many games you can play on horseback, some of them organized, some strictly informal. I mention two in their organized forms here, both accessible to the backyard horseman.

Rodeo barrel-racing is almost exclusively a woman's sport held mainly in conjunction with full-scale rodeos. Though anyone can participate, there is no such thing in the actual events as an amateur, if you think of an amateur as a slow, bumbling first-timer. Even the ten-year-old girls in this event ride like Apaches—fast and fearless—and they know exactly what they want out of that horse. The horses they ride aren't your average backyard pet either. They're bred for speed and are hot to exhibit their heritage.

This competitor is old enough to retire. But why quit if you don't feel like it? She's a tough competitor at competitive trail riding time, a good example to those of us who use our age as an excuse to be lazy.

If you intend to barrel-race in rodeos you will need a top-notch horse, good transportation, and the time to pull a lot of miles down the highway. For a dedicated few each year, however, this event does pay off in cash.

The word "O-Mok-See" refers to an organization (local, state, and national) dedicated to a standard set of games including either-sex barrel-racing and such wild events as the notorious hide race, in which a rider pulls a second person who, for reasons incomprehensible to God or man, has agreed to lay down on a stiff steerhide and have dirt scooped into his or her face at full horse-speed.

O-Mok-See events are more family-oriented than rodeo, and although competition is fierce, beginners, kids, and slow performances are all acceptable, whereas in rodeo they would be an embarrassment.

Most sound horses with some manners and speed will perform adequately in O-Mok-See events, and you can use your games horse for other events too. He will need constant tuning only if you intend to compete seriously. But there is a real danger with games horses of any kind: they begin to like the speed and excitement as much as the crowds do. Some go crazy in fact and become almost unmanageable anywhere

near an arena. Common sense, skill, and cross-country pleasure riding can prevent this kind of trouble; furthermore, if you keep your horse sane, he is less apt to injure himself and you in the heat of competition.

Endurance riding

For the backyard horseman, endurance riding or its slightly more controlled relative, competitive trail riding, is a natural. I can't say enough good about either. Endurance riding offers action, communication with the horse, time in beautiful surroundings, and the chance to learn our own and our horse's limits, all without the complex training requirements of many other events. You need a superior horse to compete for very long at this, one that is sensible, sound, and smooth-traveling, but he doesn't have to be a particular breed, size, or build. A lean, angular horse may do better because he is a more efficient traveler, but even the round and muscled horse will do well if he has the heart for the event.

No particular equipment is necessary, although you may want to invest in a specialized, lightweight endurance saddle. Although expert endurance riders monitor horse health to the point of knowing exactly what supplements are needed, basic health and feeding practices can carry you a long way in the event.

Endurance training can take place nearly anywhere: roadsides, fields, mountain trails, bike trails, dirt-surfaced race tracks, and back roads all do nicely. Once the horse begins to harden up—this may take months, depending upon what you are training for—the horse becomes a real pleasure to use simply because you can put a lot of miles on him in a hurry without doing any harm. During conditioning, you'll learn to monitor your horse's heartbeat, breathing rate, and temperature. You'll work to match speed to respiration, uphill and down. You'll recognize excessive stress from physical and attitudinal symptoms, and you'll learn how to alleviate that stress. In this event you'll really learn what makes your horse tick.

Drill teams

Maybe you like action a little less demanding and a lot more precise. Join or organize a mounted drill team. This isn't a competitive event, though I'm not sure why. It takes much careful practice and good riding habits to work out the intricate patterns.

Equipment and costumes for this activity are somewhat fancier than for many others, but not so much so as to be prohibitively expensive. You won't need an expensive horse either. He will have to be well-mannered to tolerate the action and confusion, but he won't have to endure the pounding of many others.

Neither will you. You can participate as long as you can ride. You'll travel to new places to perform. You'll have the satisfaction of working with a team, doing something to please the public. The event is complex enough to test you and your horse yet your horse will remain usable for many things besides this event. That's not a bad list.

Dressage

Of all the events for which you can school a horse, dressage, or high-schooling, is the most technically demanding and the closest thing to an art form in the horse world. The ideals behind dressage are to riding skills what the Mona Lisa is to painting, and in trying to attain those ideals all horsemen use the same brushes and colors. At its most profound level, dressage isn't competition at all: it is pure communication.

But dressage does exist apart from these

lofty heights. It exists any time horse and rider begin to understand each other well, any time there is true progress in schooling. At a high level the event itself borders on the mystical. Most of us will never attain that degree of skill, but the thought of getting there is an admirable goal for any horseman.

Even if you aren't interested in the competitive aspects of dressage, learning its fundamental methods and concepts is still an intelligent move. *The Complete Training of Horse and Rider* by Alois Podhajsky, the former director of the Spanish Riding School in Vienna and one of the premier horsemen of this century, is a superb introduction to classical training techniques, theory and maneuvers. Williamson, Jones, and Young, though primarily writing for western riders, all base their methods on dressage principles, and applying these principles has only made them better trainers of western stock and pleasure horses. Dressage principles are the common denominators underlying all good trainers' methods, western or English.

While you can learn some dressage techniques from books, if you intend to compete you'll need instruction. That instruction is widely available, and the entire field is accessible to the backyard horseman. Dressage requires a minimum of space and equipment for practice purposes. Lower-level dressage horses are highly suitable for other purposes, and nearly all horses can respond to dressage training. Your present horse can be started and taken as far as your capabilities and his limitations will allow. Then, if you want to go further, you have a good horse to sell or keep for other purposes, and you have your new skills to apply to the next horse.

There are other events both informal and organized that I haven't mentioned, not because they aren't important, but because the list of possible horseback activities is so vast. Those I've mentioned are some of the more popular among backyard horsemen.

There's an old adage: there's something about the outside of a horse that's good for the inside of a man. But that adage doesn't hold true if you just throw horses their hay and watch them age. You need to use them. Set goals, get involved, and make progress. If you do, you'll have a better horse, and you'll be a better horseman.

The deadly lurking gate-latch, waiting for an unsuspecting cinch, stirrup, or rib-cage.

chapter ten
. . . And Stay Out Of Trouble!

The troubles that come with horses vary from momentary and humorous to long term and fatal. Only one thing about horses is certain: you will have trouble. There are ways to minimize these troubles, and you can benefit by continually thinking about what might go wrong. As a friend of mine says, "when you've been around horses for a while, you see that even leading a horse through a gate has its disasters lurking."

He's right. Look at a good, strong, 4-foot gate. You lead your horse to it and push it open. As you step through, the gate swings back, slapping your horse in the chest and sending him roaring backwards, jerking the lead-rope through your fingers, burning your hide, and releasing him from his ties to you.

Maybe the gate must be pulled instead of pushed. You pull it wide and start through, but your horse decides to make one step to the side. As he does, he rams a gate latch into his ribs. He panics and jumps forward,

gouging his skin, but this rams the gate tighter into him, and in a quick fit he tears it apart. You need a new gate and maybe a veterinarian. Or, simpler and more common, he hangs up a stirrup just as he goes through. It doesn't bother his conscience one bit to give a big lunge, land on your heels, and rip the saddle apart at the same time. After a few of these episodes, you'll be looking sideways all the time to see what's out to get you.

Get rid of obvious dangers

While cows can stroll through rolls of barbed wire and never suffer a scratch, horses are a different story. Partly it's their thinner skin; partly it's the difference between the construction of their lower legs and a cow's; partly it's their volatile personalities. If there's a strand of barbed wire around, horses well get into it, and they will get hurt, often badly enough to

Patched, sagging barbed wire: a sure route to the vet.

cripple them for life. You've seen barbed-wire scars if you've looked at even a few horses. They're the gray, flaky, hairless scabs around the top of the hoof or across the chest and shoulders. Frequently, barbed wire damages the hoof-growing tissues, too, and not only is the horse scarred, but his hoof is deformed.

The solution to barbed-wire problems has two stages. The first is to repair any barbed wire on your place. Get the bottom wire up at least knee high. This will eliminate some of the injuries caused by pawing across the fence. Then be sure all wires are tight and strong. Next, use four or five strands rather than two or three. This will reduce the temptation for your horse to put his head between strands. Finally, electrify the top strand so he won't lean over it. Fence chargers cost from $20 to $60; insulators are a minor expense; electrical use is minimal.

Stage two is to get rid of all the barbed wire on your place and replace it with poles, planks, pipe, or smooth wire and electricity. If you're building horse facilities from scratch, don't use barbed wire, and you'll do just fine.

Boards and nails are another common problem. It seems no matter how you throw a board down, if it has nails in it, they'll stick up. When they do, they puncture

hooves. When hooves are punctured, your horse has serious problems. The solution: pick up any scrap lumber lying around your pastures and pens.

Anywhere there are objects protruding, up to about 7 feet above the ground, horses will bruise and cut themselves. One summer day a friend and I discovered his old rope horse with a deep gash above the eye. The only way the horse could have cut himself was to flop his head high enough to reach the metal roof-corner of his shelter, more than 6 feet above the ground. Gate and door latches; nails that have worked loose from corral rails; big slivers in planks; sharp metal corners on trailers or stock racks; overhead objects in trailers, racks, or barns; broken tree branches; anything that sticks out is a good candidate for causing a wreck.

Another place horses get into trouble is in narrow corners where a horse can easily walk in, but not so easily back out. The horse may get into these and starve or dehydrate until you find him. He may panic and destroy a bunch of the countryside getting out. He may get in head-first while fleeing an aggressive herd-mate, but continue to be abused while trapped. A yearling penned with a sour old mare died a few miles from me this way. The colt

Perhaps you own one of these. Not only are they ugly, they will sooner or later cost you at least a vet bill.

couldn't escape a narrow corner, and the old mare kicked the colt's ribs into his lungs.

A mistake that gets a lot of publicity but is still often made by beginners is leaving a halter on a horse to make him easier to catch. Horror stories are the frequent result: a faithful pack horse, turned loose after a trip to the mountains, rolls in sheer delight at being free and home. He stands to scratch himself with a shod hoof, hooks the halter with the hoof, and before the tired campers have the coffee hot, the horse has strangled.

A cagey horse is a cagey horse, and if he becomes accustomed to ducking you, he will do it when you have a halter on him too. Grab that halter, and he'll jerk it out of your hand. There are better ways of catching the horse than going out and finding him dead. Take off the halter. Take off the halter. Take off the halter.

A final, obvious precaution is to keep your gear cinched up and tight. Ropes, hobbles, slickers, anything with a loop in it, can catch on anything that protrudes and cause a wreck. Worse yet, anything with a loop in it can tie you to a bucking or runaway horse. This last item is a bit of wisdom passed down from one healthy bronc-rider to another for many generations. The others didn't believe it.

Know your animal

Serious trouble often results when riders fail to take into account what their horses don't know and then push them too hard. Here a rider is in a paradoxical position. If he doesn't push his horse, he can't know what the horse will take.

Suppose you are one of the few new owners who has actually spent a few hours handling and riding a horse before you buy him. Even with this background, you still don't know the horse's quirks, and every horse will have some. This is why it's so important to put him through the training routines discussed in chapter eight. He may pass all those tests quietly, in which case your task will be simple and enjoyable. At least you will know what to expect from there on. It isn't your horse's fault if he dumps you the first time he sees a moving vehicle if you haven't checked him out beforehand. If your horse has never loaded in a trailer before, it isn't his fault if, as you're hurrying to meet your hunting partner, he panics while loading into a dark trailer at 5:00 A.M. on a black autumn morning.

Such problems are especially common with young horses. There are going to be fights with the horse, but if, through steady

125

Big nails are handy for a lot of things—hanging bridles, ripping off ears, gouging out eyes. . . .

and intelligent use, he becomes accustomed to giving you a little more all the time, new things won't surprise him so much, and he'll be more likely to respond well. I'm not suggesting that you must always be timid about what you do on horseback. Timid riders have more trouble than bold riders do. I'm saying you have to know your horse (eventually you'll be able to generalize somewhat about all horses), and you must not push him too far.

When you do know a horse well and you see that too many situations bring poor reactions from him, stay out of further trouble by getting rid of him.

Do new training in a corral

As important as knowing the horse's limitations is the location of your efforts to discover those limitations. Anything new should be started in your corral. Things can get wooly fast even there, but at least the damage is contained. Ask yourself: has the horse done anything like this before? If he hasn't, start him in the corral.

For reasons unknown to man, horses cannot resist bashing their heads on an open barn-door. Keep these shut or tie them back against the wall.

Maintain your equipment

Chapter four dealt with maintaining equipment for economic reasons; I mention it again here as a safety factor. There's no substitute for good tools in any trade. In horsemanship your tools include saddles, headstalls, bits, blankets, pads, halters, feed bunks, trucks, trailers, shelter, gates, watering utensils, and on and on. Think about the results of your horse stepping through a worn trailer floor. Picture what happens when your horses are playing and run into the rotting poles of your pens. Picture what happens when you ask a green horse for a turn, and your bridle rein breaks.

Finding time to maintain equipment is part of having enough time to own horses. As I said in earlier chapters, if you don't have time for everything you were doing before you bought horses, you can't expect to take proper care of horses and equipment as additional chores.

Don't overestimate your own ability

The philosopher Eric Hoffer once said that naivete can be charming, but coupled with vanity, it's indistinguishable from stupidity. This applies as well to horsemanship as any other field.

We all show a degree of vanity. We look past our weaknesses and pretend they don't really exist. Until we can shake this habit, we are headed for troubles that could be avoided. I have a classy, black quarter horse colt in my breaking pen as I type this. His owner raised him from a foal, the offspring of a favorite old mare. He's friendly, smart, big, strong, and athletic. He also thinks bucking is the answer to all questions, and he is already good at it.

This colt presents me with a dilemma I've faced before. I hate to tell the owner the colt is too much for me. And who knows? In another week of ground-work he may settle down. On the other hand, I may be investing my time in a project I can't finish, and I don't charge for unfinished products. I've started a lot of colts. Most don't buck, and few that try can really buck. This one can and likes to. I've never been a good bronc rider; I'm a middle-aged schoolteacher who wishes to stay in one piece. I can send him home and swallow my pride. I can keep him with the hope he'll come around to seeing things my way. I may have to ride him, and he may hurt me. Not much for choices.

I think the dilemma illustrates the risk in overestimating our abilities. If I choose to stick with this colt, I'll have no one to blame but myself for any unpleasant consequences.

Every person who works with horses faces similar dilemmas more often than he or she would like. They may come at a point where we know what to do, but cannot accomplish it—the position I'm in with bucking horses—or they may come at a point where we simply don't know what to do next. Either way the decision we make reveals not only what we are willing to do to stay out of trouble but our attitude toward horsemanship in general. And horsemen, despite what you may have heard about the romance of taming wild steeds, there is no such thing as a horse worth getting hurt for.

Think about others

If we think about our impact on other people, we aren't necessarily avoiding the kind of trouble that leads to physical injuries. We are, however, avoiding a kind of trouble that can curtail our enjoyment of horses. When your horse walks through your poor fences and destroys a neighbor's new lawn, there may be more than a few hundred dollars' damage; the incident may begin a permanent hatred of horse owners. Being likable, helpful, and responsible as horsemen isn't allowing the world to walk all over us; it's just good public relations.

Be careful on the road

When hauling horses, avoid trouble by driving extra carefully. Corner slowly, tap your brakes a few times before stopping or slowing. Horses can stand well for turns or stops if they are warned, but surprises make them scramble or fall. Check your equipment frequently. Even the best trailer hitch can come undone. And drive defensively. Since you can't react nearly as fast with a load of livestock as without, you must drive way out in front of yourself, and you must drive for all the others on the highway.

Finally if you need to hoist a few on your way home from horse events, hoist soft drinks. Even a couple of beers can fuzz your judgment. You've invested all that time, money, and emotion in your horses; don't take frivolous chances with them.

Ol' Buck—in the horse world the epitome of the retired gentleman. He has roped a thousand calves, babysat the kids, packed hunters' equipment, snubbed rank horses, provided mannerly company for new horses on the place. In terms of ability and accomplishment, he is beyond price.
But his teeth are gone; his knees, knobby with calcium. On the best of pasture he can't eat enough to keep his ribs from showing. No one knows anymore how old he is. Winter wears him down to a skeleton. Ol' Buck—a horseman's ethical dilemma.

chapter eleven

When The Handwriting Is On The Wall

Once we've owned horses for a time, we aren't very good at parting with them, even when it becomes obvious that parting is just what we should do. Sometimes this doesn't hurt anything; sometimes neglect and suffering result. The sad fact is that no matter now much we wish to believe otherwise, the day will come when we must separate ourselves from our horses. There are many reasons this might happen; each reason comes with its own special circumstances. Each takes careful thought, and the final decision may be a heartbreaker. But honest horsemanship demands that we think and decide.

Let's begin with the inevitable: old age. Assuming your horse gets there quicker than you do, what will you do when you suddenly realize he's no longer thirteen, he's twenty-three? He may still be healthy, but his working days are numbered.

Your choices aren't easy. You can put him through the sale ring, but it's almost certain he will end as a canner. You can sell him to

someone else, but you don't control his future that way either. He really isn't attractive to a buyer anyway. You can keep feeding him until he dies, but that could be seven days or seven years. You can have him put to sleep, but you could be shortening his lifespan by years.

Your choices are similar with a crippled horse. An injured gelding is worthless to anyone and will surely be a canner. No one on the horse market wants him either. He could be put to sleep, but maybe he doesn't like the idea any better than you do. A crippled mare is different in that she has the ability to breed well into her twenties. But if the crippling is a result of poor conformation, or if she has always had a questionable disposition, you shouldn't risk perpetuating her faults. I heard a "mule-man" lament once that no one brought top-quality mares to the big, gentle jack he had as stud. Instead, owners brought undesirable mares, then blamed the jack when the offspring were mean or poorly built. You don't want to add to the pet pollution problem by indiscriminate breeding.

Another reason for parting with a horse is that he is unsuited to your needs. He is too big, too small, too well-trained, or too hard to handle. It's surprising how many unsuitable horses people keep. Again it's often a matter of vanity. We hate to admit we aren't in control of the situation. Yet even among accomplished horsemen there are horses that "have the sign" on a rider, and the rider admits his fear or distaste. No one thinks the less of the rider for it. Backyard horsemen need to learn the lesson.

Perhaps money is your problem. It's pretty common for household expenses to exceed income. This kind of trouble can destroy your relationships with people as well as with horses, and the hope of horsemanship is not enough reason to allow this to happen. In addition, when the budget is crumbling, the horse may suffer too, whether from short feed or short tempers. Be honest with yourself. Sell the horses and trailer; get back on your financial feet. If you can't like yourself, you won't like the horse much either. Going through this problem is no disgrace. Some of the world's wealthiest people have spent too much on horses. You'll be in good company.

If moving to a new home or changing jobs means you're leaving the horses a day's drive behind, if there is no remedy in sight, you should probably part with them for this reason too. If the move is for family or career improvement, these are more important than your horses. If you think "my horse means more to me than people do," you'd better find an analyst along with your new home.

Assuming that a dedicated backyard horseman's skills improve rapidly, what happens when the horse who has served you faithfully for several years isn't enough horse any more? Do you dump him? Do you feed him for no purpose while you work a new horse?

Two more unhappy, but common, possibilities are the encroachment of city on your land and changes in zoning regulations. In many cases there will be little you can do except sell your horses, though in some cities, horsemen have joined together to forestall their own extinction. If you can't handle petty political conflict you're out of luck, because there are no miracles where urban sprawl is concerned. Shopping malls, golf courses, and baseball fields will have hundreds of supporters for every one of us horse people.

All of these prospects and more face horse-people every day. Some owners face the problems realistically and do the responsible thing. Others don't, and their horses stand unused and unwanted, often in poor conditions. While horses aren't suffering physical pain in most of these cases—though in some they are—remember the romance we have with the species comes from the horse's abilty to perform. When a horse can't work, we don't think much of it, and this may lead to neglect. Furthermore, the longer we neglect an animal, the less valuable it is to a potential buyer.

Your choices are limited and relatively severe, but there are choices.

The first consideration with aged or crippled animals should be having them put to sleep. It's no kindness to leave an animal stand in severe pain for years when the one sure thing we all know about animal or human life is that it isn't permanent. We have a duty to make the best decision we can about living pain versus painless death. And the death is painless if done right. Veterinarians know how to put a horse down just as they know how to save animal lives. A bullet is more crude but just as good. We watch human murders impassively each week on TV, but we recoil from the death of an animal.

I once executed a yearling colt that had tried unsuccessfully to scramble over a high corral. Her back was broken, her screams were hideous, and her efforts to move paralyzed rear legs heartbreaking. I didn't enjoy pulling the trigger, but it had to be done. The spectators—a whole corral-rail full of guests—told me I was the cruelest person they knew. I've never understood their thinking and never doubted my own action in that instance.

The most controversial way to get rid of horses is through the canner markets. No doubt the horror stories of canners being poorly treated have some basis in fact. But then so do some of the horror stories wafting from individual owners' yards. The truth is the canner market does the horse world a real service. Without it every sick, mean, crippled, useless horse would still be taking up space and feed, and there would be several thousand more of them each week across the nation. There is simply no other workable way of culling in the horse world.

But canning a beautiful, defenseless horse, you say? How cruel! How inhumane!

I ask you in return: do you eat beef? Tell me those frisky, shiny, fat, little red calves with the big eyes, whisking tails and noses wet with drops of milk still on the chin whiskers are somehow a less delightful creation than a horse, somehow more deserving of an early death. Go sit in the corner of a pig-pen and watch half-grown porkers with their slick bodies, their endless conversation of squeals and grunts, their insatiable curiosity, their sense of humor, their sheer silliness at play, their fastidious efforts to use just one spot as a toilet. Let them oink and cavort around you and then tell me if they are somehow a less delightful creation than a horse.

Less romantic, yes. Cows and pigs haven't carried handsome cowboys or knights in armor or naked long-haired ladies in cologne commercials. But less delightful as part and parcel of the earth? I doubt it. Surely ol' Buttercup, the smooth brown Shorthorn-Jersey who followed my kids and approached any visitor hoping for a scratching, who delivered three gallons of rich milk from the day she freshened, surely Buttercup was a pet too, perhaps even more than the horses, which were expected to be useful and unobtrusive.

We horsemen have let our emotions run wild on the subject of canners. True, if you can avoid it, the canner market is no place for a faithful animal, no place for the kids' pet of ten years even if this is the last chance for some economic return. You don't can your friends. But a lot of people don't can their enemies either. They get bucked off, kicked, bitten, eaten out of house and home. The whole horse-experience turns into a

nightmare. And they wring their hands over what to do. It's simple. If your horse is a cull, cull him.

What happens? The horse is trucked to a slaughter house. His care may be minimal, but so is the time spent. There's an investment here that must be protected. Abusive care and weight loss mean money lost, so it isn't likely such things will happen often. When the appointed day comes, the horse is killed with a stun-gun just as cattle and pigs are. His entire carcass is turned into products useful to humans in some way, often including food. Yes, there is probably carelessness. No, the whole things isn't as neat as the vet's needle. But this is an industry that operates as efficiently as possible. Needless brutalities aren't the rule.

I'm not advocating canning as the simple way out of one's responsibilities. I do say that canning horses is legitimate, that it does a service for the horse world, that it doesn't deserve all the bad press it gets. It certainly is no more cruel than the life some horses live in the hands of neglectful owners.

You may never need to use the canner market. If you have a good, usable horse, the sale ring may still be the place to go. Particularly in spring and early summer, people just like yourself are looking for good horses. You can insist the horse sell with saddle-stock rather than with the loose animals (those that won't get a serious bid because there is no information about their age, breeding, and training). You can ride your horse in the ring or have a ring attendant do it for a small fee. If you have the horse cleaned up and acting right, if you can give the auctioneer a list of the horse's attributes, he may just sell well. Remember the more he sells for, the more the auctioneer makes. Do your part, and the auctioneer will be on your side.

Who gets the horse? Not the canners if you don't allow it. Guest ranches buy horses. Outfitters are always looking for good quiet horses. Speculators buy horses they think they can take east or west and sell for a better price. And backyard horsemen buy horses too. But whoever buys him, once he leaves the grounds you have no more to say about your horse.

If you don't like the gamble of the sale ring, gamble on the open market. Advertise in the newspapers, and spend enough money to make the horse sound valuable. "For sale, one brown horse" isn't good enough. People want to know age, size, disposition, training, breeding, experience, and price. The quick, cheap ad suggests

you're ashamed of your horse, or perhaps hiding something about him. I answered an ad once for what sounded like an excellent buy, only to find out by accident—I never did see the horse—that the horse was crippled by barbed wire. This last fact had somehow never been mentioned either in the ad or in phone calls.

It's hard to know what price to ask for your horse. You'll need to compare him to advertised prices of other horses with similar attributes. You can also ask other horsemen about prices in your area. You may make money over your initial investment, and you may not. Regardless, the money you've spent for feed and care makes the horse a losing proposition anyway if you're looking at him strictly in economic terms. Don't feel bad if you lose a few hundred dollars at sale time.

If the horse you're selling is just plain nasty, you must change your approach. Be honest. If you think the horse is more than you can handle but you think someone else may make him work, advertise that way. "He's too much for me, but a good, sound horse for an experienced rider, price negotiable" is better than a list of qualities that don't matter or don't exist. Outright lies could bring you a lawsuit or, worse, hurt someone who thought you had an honest face. "Let the seller be honest" is a more useful adage than "Let the buyer beware."

One avenue that isn't traveled enough by horse owners is the barter system. Trade your horse for a boat, take a ride in the boat, then sell it. Of course you could be taken for a real ride if the articles you trade for are defective, but the new horse owner is taking the same chance.

Still another possibility is to give the horse away, not quite for free, but for a small price, say $50. You might try this approach with an older horse, which is no longer able to keep up for you but which would do well for kids. The small fee keeps people from feeling obligated to you, but it also allows you to be pretty snoopy about what kind of care the horse will get. Be careful. Some kids will love that old horse and treat him right. Others will run him to death.

That about sums up your options. A new home, a bullet or needle, years of uselessness, a trip to the canners . . . doesn't sound very cheerful, does it? But actions have consequences. You certainly didn't assume the horse would magically wing it's way heavenward at an apppointed time. Not really.

chapter twelve
Rewards Of Horsemanship

By now if you're still with me, you've a pretty good idea what small scale horsemanship entails, but you don't yet have the payoff. That payoff isn't dollars, nor is it any of the material things we generally reward ourselves with. The payoff from horsemanship is subtle and long in coming, so much so that many people may not see it. You see, the rewards of horsemanship are mainly intrinsic and intangible rather than extrinsic, concrete, or visible. If you can't be happy with such quiet, personal satisfaction, horses will probably never really please you.

Let's say you've plunged into the horse business, and you've been honest about it. You've purchased equipment carefully, planned and built a decent facility, bought a well-broke horse or two. Furthermore, you've made sure your horse has good manners in all kinds of situations, and you've had some success in teaching those manners yourself. Let's say you've made a tentative start in something technical and

specific—jumping for example. Your horse is doing what he's told; you haven't taken any terminal falls yet; you've even got a third-place novice-jumper's ribbon. Your horse is healthy and comfortable. You're enjoying the ownership. You've learned to spot the most obvious disasters before they happen. You recognize your horse's personality quirks, and you've learned to live with them. Let's say you've accomplished just what this book suggests—with the aid of other reading material, some expert advice along the way, and hours of experience on your own. Just what are you getting out of all this, and what will you get in the future?

One of the more obvious rewards, one you've noticed on your own, is that working with horses is simply fun. Fun is among the most elementary rewards, the aspect of horsemanship that kids often confuse with horsemanship itself, the aspect that provides so many good memories for us all. And though it is an elementary reward, it is also the foundation for everything else. If there were no fun in it, horsemanship would die.

But simply having fun isn't enough motivation or reward to keep us going forever, because as we age our definition of fun changes. Fun when I was sixteen meant a jousting contest with my brothers, charging horseback across the fields, throwing crab apples instead of sticking each other with lances. Fun was jumping aboard a horse as he was turned loose after a ride and hanging on without bridle or saddle while he pounded out to the lakeside pasture to join the rest of his herd. Fun was racing the last two miles home and turning mid-gallop to see my brother's loosened cinches waving in the air. Nowadays I keep going with horses quite happily without being on the edge of disaster.

A second reward, also basic to the whole undertaking, is the horse himself. Despite all I've said about him being a rather slow-witted beast capable of vast trouble-making, he is after all just what misty-eyed romantics see him as: a pretty noble animal, at least when he's at his best. He appeals to our sense of beauty and to our emotions. He evokes our love of those who give something extra and our admiration of those who perform necessary or exciting things with class. We see in good horses the best attributes of humanity. But whatever it is we see, the horse as nothing more than a horse appeals to us and rewards us. I like walking among my horses on a cold moonlit night, listening to them munch hay, listening to the crunch of their hooves on snow-covered ground. I like watching them race ahead of a cold autumn breeze. Do you realize how long they've been doing that stuff, how many winter nights they've endured to keep the species alive for our use?

A third reward is more complex. I'll call it fulfillment. In our efforts to become horsemen we learn about, expand and fulfill ourselves. We learn our present abilities and limits, surpass these, see new possibilities, and succeed at these too. I doubt true horsemanship can begin until this expansion of self emerges as part of what we are doing. I doubt that ownership alone can help you know yourself, but horsemanship can.

For example, a beginner watches an accomplished horseman take a good horse through a series of lead changes, smooth back-ups, hard stops, side passes, and roll-backs. One beginner might envy the horseman's skill without understanding how the skill was attained. Another beginner may feel jealousy, in which case the beginner rationalizes: "Sure he just had some rich guy train the horse to do all that useless stuff; that stuff ain't no good for a mountain horse anyway."

The jealous person probably never will understand what he is looking at unless something unusual jars him out of his narrow-mindedness. He's the same person who will continue using what little he knows about horses with no questions, no progress, and little success. In many cases his horses will suffer more for his ignorance than the owner will.

The envious person, however, may decide that he too can do what the horseman is doing and begin to attain those skills. When this happens, this beginner will change. He will learn how some complex things are done, and he will learn that he himself can do them. He'll learn about himself as well as about the skills.

Part of fulfillment shows in our pride in good facilities, equipment, and skills, things that are apparent to others. Elsewhere I've mentioned a horse named Gus. He's a superior horse, superior in looks, intelligence, and ability. Other horsemen watching him work see he's superior, and his superiority reflects on me as a horseman.

But such fulfillment is easily perverted. It's easy to become boastful; it is easy to confuse a wall of trophies with horsemanship itself. While owning the right gear and knowing the right things are part of the reward, mistaking these outward signs for the intangible essence may even diminish us in the eyes of other people. Who can blame them for their skepticism if we sparkle with the right words and costumes but fade in performance?

A fourth reward comes with kids and horses. In chapter one I wrote negatively about this relationship because it so often fails. But in many cases it succeeds wonderfully. Horses can contribute greatly to a child's developing sense of responsibility, to his compassion, and to his self-confidence, particularly when parents plug along behind the scenes to help their child succeed. When this happens, horses are a reward for the whole family, a source of pride in children's accomplishments, a focus of common activity on something long term, productive, and intelligent. Particularly for girls, horses can be true friends during adolescence. Girls also seem, more often than boys, to become competent horsemen at this age. Plenty of boys become competent riders, but it's girls who care more about what the horse is than what the horse can do for them.

Reward number five is a neat little side-effect: horses can bring you closer to people. As my own kids have noticed, if you have horses, you'll have friends. Kids who would ignore you will love your horse and accept you as an extension of the horse. Passers-by will wave at you when you're mounted but ignore you if you're walking. In February 1985, *Horseman Magazine* ran an article about Houston police using horses: one of the officers involved was quoted: "People love horses. They will come up and pet the horse and talk to officers."

I was lying up in the shade late one day before packing into the wilderness the next, and a family of campers brought kids over to pet my horses. The two small children stayed for an hour while the mother told me of the family's desire to move out of town, of their wish to have horses, of the need for kids to have animals, of her own high times riding as a child. My horses broke down the natural distrust between strangers, provided the topic for conversation, and fueled that family's dream.

The sixth and last reward is the least tangible, the most complex, and, in its many possible forms, possibly the highest. It is also the most difficult to express.

I recall a short hunting trip—just three of us: me, my long-time hunting partner Bob, and my son Jeff. We came out of the woods in the dark. The first snows had melted and the second not yet come. The temperature was mild, the air damp, the sky black and clearing. I was comfortably warm, and Gus was hustling right along. I rode a heavy, utilitarian saddle, not the best, but good; I pulled a packhorse that would quietly carry all I could ever ask, wherever I might ask. Jeff rode a good little gray whose short legs pump smoothly and fast enough to keep the big horses nodding to keep up. Bob was right behind, comfortable too, on a big roping horse, with good equipment and the knowledge he had power and common sense under his saddle.

We weren't mountain men coming into winter camp. We weren't kidding anyone, not even ourselves, that we were. We were a teacher, his son, and a businessman riding a

logging road in a second-growth forest a few safe miles from home. But it didn't matter. There was a feeling there of good horses and good equipment and a good day passing even if Jeff had missed a big buck. I felt peacefulness or satisfaction, but those words don't capture it either. Quality, perhaps, if we define quality as a feeling rather than a value, quality that came with the horses and was somehow wrapped up in their presence. I suspect that successful dressage riders, endurance riders, and many others get the same feeling. We see the same quality in the arts, where the artist, in trying to capture a particular quality of life, becomes a part of that quality.

That quality is the sixth reward of horsemanship. After a time horsemanship isn't any longer what I have or what I can do. Horsemanship becomes part of what I am. And when it has gone that far it is a force and a quality rather than a possession.

It's this quality of horsemanship that I've been driving at throughout this book. It's this quality, or feeling, or whatever it is, that will bring you continuing satisfaction with horses long after the initial excitement and romance have faded into reality. It is this quality that will make you continue learning and growing as a horseman.

Whether you get to this sixth reward or not depends a great deal more on you and your attitudes than it does on this book, though I hope the book will help. I hope you and many other horse owners will attain that lofty title: horseman.

Further Reading

Chapter 1
Happy Horsemanship by Dorothy
    Henderson Pinch (Arco Publishing,
    1966).
*How to Stay Out of Trouble With Your
    Horse* by Walter Farley (Doubleday and
    Co., 1981).
"Too Much TLC" by Martha B. Jacob (*The
    Western Horseman*, July, 1984).

Chapter 2
"Lush is no mistake" by Chris Cooper
    (*Horseman Magazine*, August 1984).
"No Impact Horse Packing" by Tom Bryant
    (*The Western Horseman*, August, 1984).

Chapter 3
"Understanding Bits" by Greg Darnall
    (*Horseman Magazine*, May and June,
    1984).
"Saddle Safety" by Ric Rudolph (*The
    Western Horseman*, October 1985).

Chapter 4
Series of four articles on trailering in *The
    Western Horseman*, June, 1984.

Chapter 5
How to Buy the Right Horse by Margaret
    Cabell Self (The Farnam Horse Library).
"Tips on Buying a Horse" by Elaine
    Swanson (*The Western Horseman*,
    September, 1984).
"Never Buy a Bonfire" by Nancy Bowker
    (*Horseman Magazine*, June 1984).

Chapter 6
Western Horse Behavior and Training by
    Robert W. Miller (Dolphin Books, 1975).
Understanding Horse Psychology edited by
    Bill Weikel (Farnam Horse Library).

Chapter 7
Veterinary Notes for Horse Owners by Capt.
    M. Horace Hayes (Arco, 1968). This is
    the most comprehensive of the
    veterinary guides listed here.
Horse Ailments and Health Care by Colin
    Vogel (Arco, 1982).
A Veterinary Guide for Animal Owners by
    C. E. Spaulding (Rodale Press, 1976).
The Complete Horseshoeing Guide by
    Robert F. Wiseman (University of
    Oklahoma Press, 1968).
"Don't Ride a Sore-backed Hoss" by Buster
    McLaury (*The Western Horseman*, June
    1985).
"The Beginnings of Colic" by Robert M.
    Miller (*The Western Horseman*,
    October, 1984).
"Keeping Show Horses Healthy (Parts I &
    II)" (*The Western Horseman*, Jan. & Feb.
    1985).
"Step Up and Ride," an article about
    exercise for pregnant mares by Linda
    Blake (*The Western Horseman*, Feb.
    1985).

Chapter 8

The Schooling of the Horse by John Richard Young (University of Oklahoma Press, 1982). This is a newly revised version of the book formerly known as *The Schooling of the Western Horse*. It is one of the best general works available to American horsemen.

"How's and Why's of a Well-Broke Horse" by Mike Craig (*The Western Horseman*, February, 1985).

"Training the Green Western Pleasure Horse" by Lynda Bloom (*The Western Horseman*, February, 1985).

"Backing" by Connie S. Reynolds (*The Western Horseman*, October, 1984).

"Turning on the Forehand" by Connie S. Reynolds (*The Western Horseman*, August, 1984).

"How to Avoid Driving Dangers" by Kathy Hansen (*The Western Horseman*, April, 1985).

"Will Your Horse Step Inside?" by Emilie Cartoun (*Horseman Magazine*, December, 1984).

"Hey, Kid! Come Along for the Ride" by Leslie Mayer (*Horseman Magazine*, March, 1985).

"Welcome, New Friend" by Lucie Stigler (*Horseman Magazine*, June, 1984).

"Grow, You Mental Midget" by Hunter Pen (*Horseman Magazine*, July, 1984).

"Life Before the First Ride" by Cori Deyoe (*Horseman Magazine*, December, 1984).

"Keeping Them Sensible" by Pat Close (*The Western Horseman*, April 1985).

Chapter 9

Horses, Hitches, and Rocky Trails by Joe Back (Swallow Press, 1959).

Packin' In On Mules and Horses by Smoke Elser and Bill Brown (Mountain Press, 1980).

Techniques and Equipment for Wilderness Horse Travel (U.S. Forest Service, Equipment Development Center, Missoula, MT 1984).

Calf Roping by Roy Cooper (The Western Horseman, 1984).

Team Roping by Leo Camarillo (The Western Horseman, 1982).

Breaking and Training the Stock Horse by Charles O. Williamson (available by writing 105 Oak Circle, Grants Pass, Oregon 97526).

Reining by Al Dunning (The Western Horseman, 1983).

The Complete Book of Show Jumping by Michael Clayton and William Steinkraus (Crown Publishers, 1975).

The Complete Training of Horse and Rider by Alois Podhajsky (Doubleday & Co. 1965). A superb introduction to classical horsemanship by the former director of the Spanish Riding School.

Dressage for Beginners by R. L. V. French Blake (Houghton Mifflin 1973).

The USCTA Book of Eventing edited by Sally O'Connor (Addison-Wesley Publishing, 1982).

Games on Horseback by Chan Bergen (Western Horseman Books, 1967).

"Team Roping: First Things First" by Allan Byrd (*The Western Horseman*, November 1984).

"Pleasure Driving" by Lynda Bloom (*The Western Horseman*, November 1984).

"Amateur: Status of the Non-Pro Horseman" (*Horseman Magazine*, June 1984).

Chapter 11

"Selling a Horse" by C. K. Cash (*The Western Horseman*, January 1985).

"Selling Your Horse at an Auction" by Lynda Bloom (*The Western Horseman*, August 1984).

Index